CW00530291

WOLVERHAMPTON RAILWAYS

THROUGH TIME

Mike Hitches

AMBERLEY PUBLISHING

First published 2011

Amberley Publishing
The Hill, Stroud
Gloucestershire, GL5 4EP

www.amberley-books.com

Copyright © Mike Hitches, 2011

The right of Mike Hitches to be identified as the
Author of this work has been asserted in accordance
with the Copyrights, Designs and Patents Act 1988.

ISBN 978 1 84868 655 7

All rights reserved. No part of this book may be
reprinted or reproduced or utilised in any form
or by any electronic, mechanical or other means,
now known or hereafter invented, including
photocopying and recording, or in any information
storage or retrieval system, without the permission
in writing from the Publishers.

British Library Cataloguing in Publication Data.
A catalogue record for this book is available from
the British Library.

Typeset in 9.5pt on 12pt Celeste.
Typesetting by Amberley Publishing.
Printed in the UK.

Introduction

Wolverhampton first appeared on the railway map when the Grand Junction Railway's line between Liverpool and Birmingham, via Bescot, opened in 1837. Its route passed through Wolverhampton, but the town was viewed as relatively unimportant at the time and was served by a small station at an inconvenient location. This station was titled Wednesfield Heath from 1852. From this rather insignificant beginning, Wolverhampton was to become one of the more important railway towns in Britain and was destined to see a great deal of political manoeuvring and corporate 'dirty tricks', most of which would be illegal today and could put directors behind bars. Several companies vied with one another to become the most important to serve the town and its growing industrial base, thereby gaining profit from the vast industrial wealth that was being generated in the nearby Black Country, through its coal mines, ironworks and factories (virtually all have now gone from the landscape). The result of this competition was that two major railway stations served the town, along with smaller ones in the Black Country, several goods yards to deal with huge quantities of freight traffic emanating from Black Country and Wolverhampton industries, and an important locomotive and construction works. The works always maintained Great Western locomotives, having been originally built by the Shrewsbury and Birmingham Railway but coming under GWR control after the little Shrewsbury company had been absorbed into the Paddington company. The town also housed three locomotive sheds at Stafford Road, Oxley (of the GWR) and at Bushbury, which was built by the London and North Western Railway, the GJR forming part of the Euston company.

Although never envisaged by the GJR, Wolverhampton became an important railway junction as rival companies built their lines into the town. By 1854, there were junctions at Stafford Road, where the little S&B met the GWR; Bushbury, where the Oxford, Worcester Railway met the GJR route between Birmingham and Stafford; Cannock Road, where the OW&W left the GWR to link up with the GJR at Bushbury; and at Priestfield, where the GWR's Birmingham, Wolverhampton and Dudley Railway joined the OW&W from Stourbridge and Dudley in order to gain access to Wolverhampton itself.

Development of Wolverhampton as an important railway centre derived from bitter rivalry between companies fighting for routes from London and the West Midlands to Merseyside. The town became a crucible of conflict when the ambitious Shrewsbury and Birmingham Railway was curtailed at Wolverhampton and two routes to Birmingham, which were to create a direct link to London, were approved by parliament. The latter generated fierce competition between two companies who had never been on friendly terms; the LNWR, whose Stour Valley line linked Birmingham New Street with a High Level station at Wolverhampton, and the GWR, who built the broad-gauge BW&DR from Birmingham Snow Hill to Wolverhampton Low Level station. Construction of the GWR broad gauge from Paddington, creeping north to Birmingham and Wolverhampton and hopefully to Merseyside, did little to calm LNWR fears that the 7-foot gauge would eventually reach its goal, the Euston company having made many futile attempts to prevent encroachment of the broad gauge into its territory, all of which added fuel to the conflict. Indeed, the broad gauge only ever reached Wolverhampton; takeover of the standard-gauge Shrewsbury & Birmingham Railway made any extension of the 7-foot gauge futile. Yet another ingredient to add to the furnace at Wolverhamton was the development of the OW&W who, initially, were on good terms with the GWR and its broad-gauge interests, only later to turn against them and try to forge an alliance with their bitter enemy, the LNWR. This caused the GWR some grief because had the OW&W joined forces with Euston, then the GWR would have had problems gaining access to Wolverhampton and it could have killed any prospect of reaching Merseyside and sharing in the lucrative export markets and imports at the major seaport at Liverpool. The matter was only finally resolved when the OW&W could not complete its line and parliament allowed the GWR to finish it.

When these disputes were finally settled, two companies operated around Wolverhampton, the LNWR and GWR, the Euston company becoming part of the London, Midland and Scottish Railway at the 1923 'Grouping'. The GWR retained its name right up to nationalisation in 1948. Even in the early years of State ownership, two regions still operated trains at Wolverhampton: London Midland Region operating services to High Level, and Western Region operating Low Level services, but this was to change in the 1960s, with major consequences for what was the substantial GWR system. Under modernisation, the West Coast Main Line was to be fully electrified, which meant the High Level line at Wolverhampton would be so treated and a new High Level station was to be built. While electrification was in progress services were concentrated on Low Level, but once all was complete, the old GWR station was reduced to operating local services between Birmingham Snow Hill and Wolverhampton, while all express services went to High Level. By 1972 the line between Snow Hill and Low Level was closed. The station itself was to become a Grade II listed building and still stands. The line from Snow Hill was reopened in the twenty-first century as a tram system but does not now go to Low Level but to the centre of Wolverhamton at a new station called Wolverhampton St George. Since the privatisation of the railways under the Conservative government of Margaret Thatcher, several operators run mainline services at High Level, including Virgin Pendelino trains to and from Euston and Scotland. Virgin also runs its CrossCountry services through Wolverhampton. London Midland now runs local services to Birmingham and Shrewsbury, and Arriva Trains Wales operate services between Birmingham International and Holyhead, via High Level and Shrewsbury. Thus, despite some decline in train services at Wolverhampton, there is still much to see on the railway here.

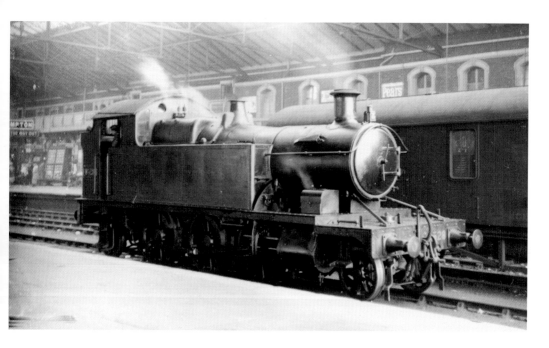

Wolverhampton Low Level Station

GWR Churchward 2-6-2 Prairie Tank No. 4528 with inside steam pipes and French built 4-4-2 Atlantic No. 104 *Alliance* at Wolverhampton Low Level station in 1924. Although finally becoming the property of the GWR, the station was originally owned by the three companies who shared its facilities, and the engineers of these three companies shared in its design. The station buildings were designed by John Fowler of Oxford, Worcester and Wolverhampton Railway, the roof by I. K. Brunel of the GWR and the track and platform layout were devised by Henry Robertson of the Shrewsbury & Birmingham Railway. By the mid-1850s all three companies were merged together all being part of the Paddington company.

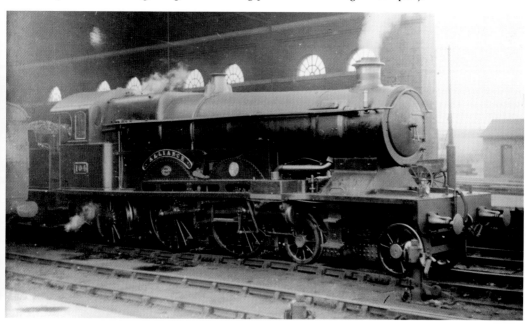

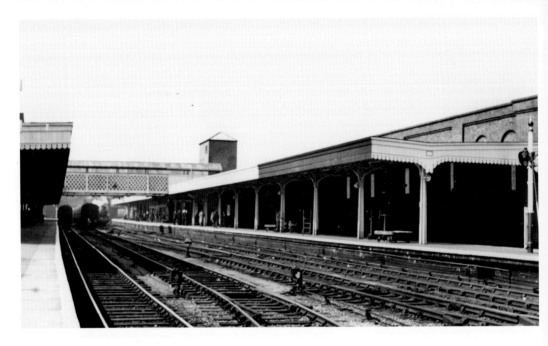

The Dismantling of Low Level Station

Above is Low Level station in the 1930s after its overall roof had been removed. By the 1923 'Grouping', the 575-foot-long iron and glass roof which weighed 400 tons was suffering from serious corrosion, despite repairs having been carried out over the years, leaving the GWR with little choice but to remove it. On 2 October work began on dismantling the roof and it was completed by early May 1934, with little interruption to traffic. Standard GWR canopies were placed over the platforms as work progressed. Below, ex-GWR Castle Class 4-6-0 No. 5065 *Newport Castle* is seen at Low Level with a southbound express in late 1950s.

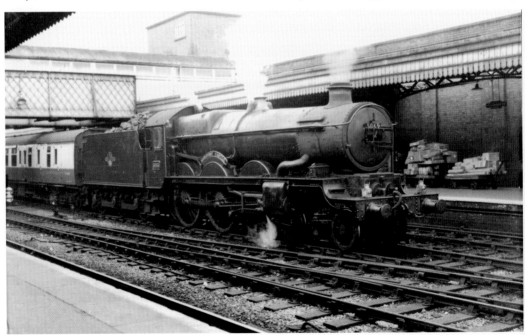

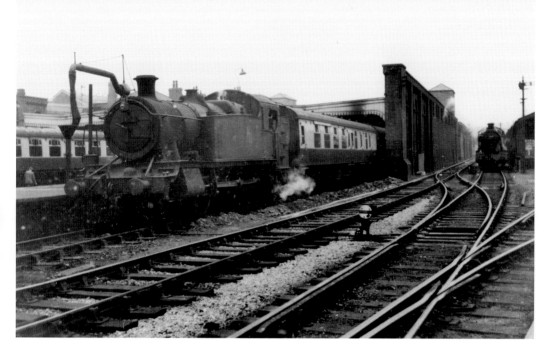

GWR Churchward 2-6-2 Prairie Tank

GWR Churchward 2-6-2 Prairie tank No. 3102 waits in the bay with empty stock in the late 1950s. Below is an ex-GWR side corridor coach, built in 1913, at Low Level station in 1960. Unusually, the coach was fitted with American-style bogies.

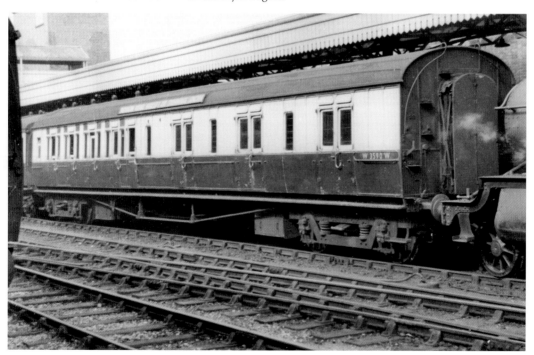

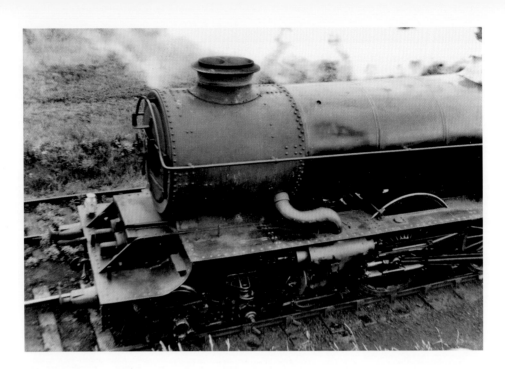

King Edward V

Waiting in the sidings at Low Level station is the largest of all the GWR express engines, the famous Collett King Class 4-6-0s, No. 6016 *King Edward V*, having just brought in an express from Paddington. These engines were often used on Paddington–Birmingham expresses and Wolverhampton always had a few allocated here. Below, at Low Level, is a view of the intermediate 3,500-gallon tender attached to No. 7821 *Ditcheat Manor* on a Down express. Wednesfield Road bridge can be seen in the background.

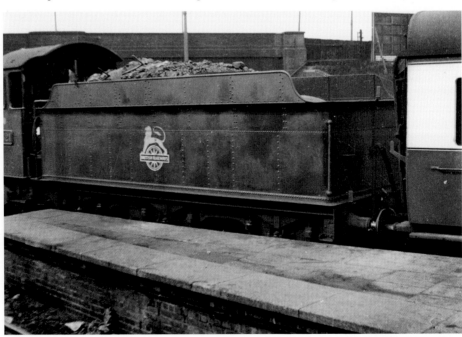

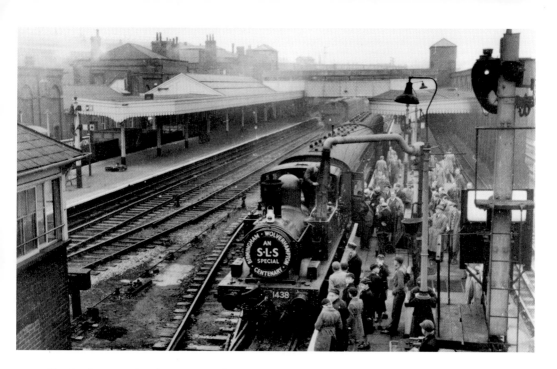

Birmingham, Wolverhampton and Dudley Railway Centenary

Above, ex-GWR Collett 0-4-2T No. 1438 is at the head of a Stephenson's Locomotive Society special from Low Level to Birmingham Snow Hill on 13 November 1954 as part of the celebrations for the centenary of the Birmingham, Wolverhampton and Dudley Railway. Below, near to Low Level station, with an ex-GWR loco. behind are a rake of ex-LMS Reid composite coaches, the bars across the droplights having been fitted for use on the rather distant Maryport and Carlisle line. The old Midland Railway line to Walsall can be seen in the background.

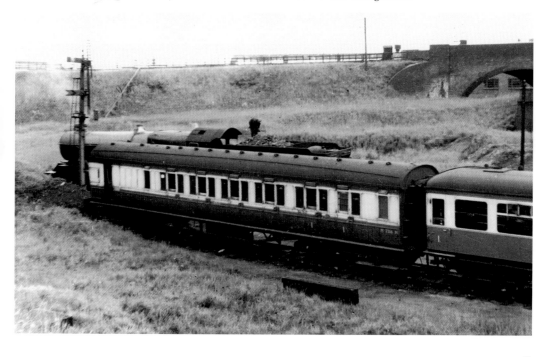

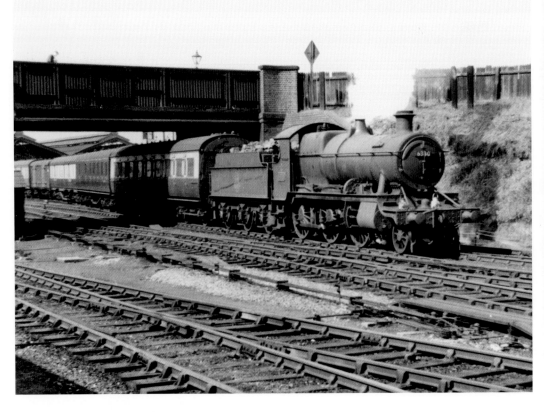

Ex-Churchward 2-6-0 No. 6340
Two views of ex-Churchward 2-6-0 No. 6340 at Low Level in the 1950s. The upper view shows an Up parcels train in 1956, with the carriage shed in the background, while the lower view shows the same engine marshalling coaching stock.

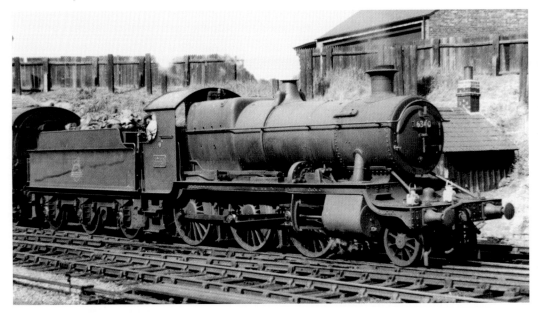

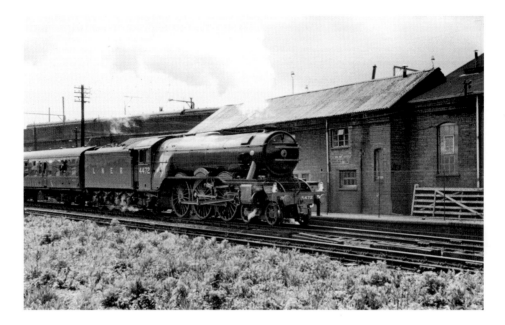

Flying Scotsman

As steam began to decline in the mid-1960s, many steam excursions were run. In the upper picture, ex-LNER Gresley's famous *Flying Scotsman* in 1930s livery, numbered 4472 and painted in the LNER apple green, is seen passing through Low Level station with an excursion for Ruabon and Porthmadog, probably a Festiniog Railway Society special, on 9 May 1965. Replacements for steam traction are already present on 9 May 1965 as a pair of English Electric Type 4 1Co-Co1 locos (later Class 40) No. D213 pilots No. D221 on a Snow Hill to Blackpool train. As can be seen in both views, electrification is continuing apace at the High Level station, which would bring about the decline of the old GWR line and explains why the train to the north-west is running through Low Level. It will gain the ex-LNWR line at Bushbury Junction.

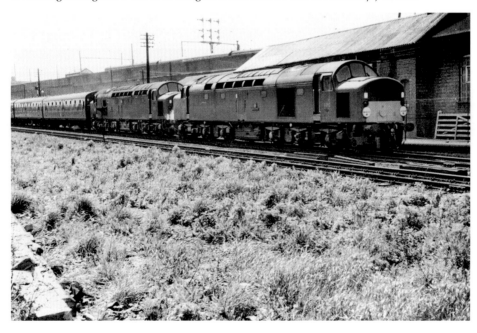

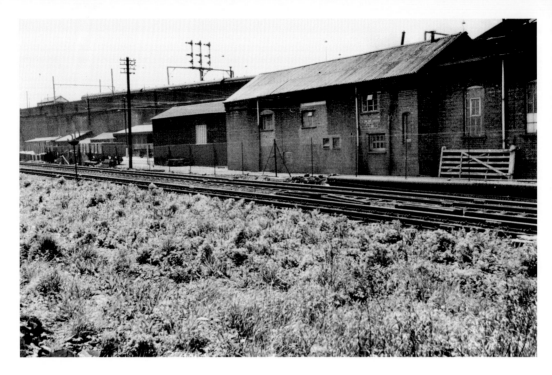

Low Level Station

The above view shows the cluster of buildings on the west side of the ex-GWR line just north of Low Level station in 1965. The lower view shows the complex of lines at the Birmingham end at Low Level showing the GWR tunnels on the BW&D line with a relieving arch above and a push-pull trailer in the siding on the right. On the embankment is the ex-LNWR Wolverhampton No. 1 signal box and the connection to the ex-Midland Railway line at Heath Town Junction on the left.

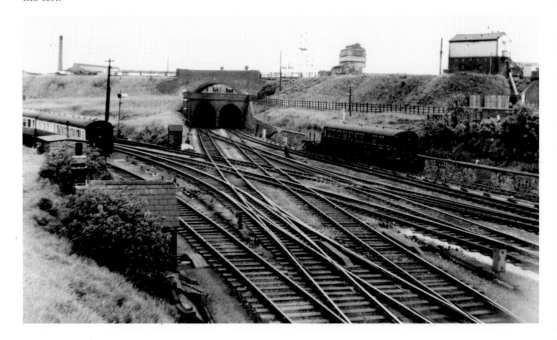

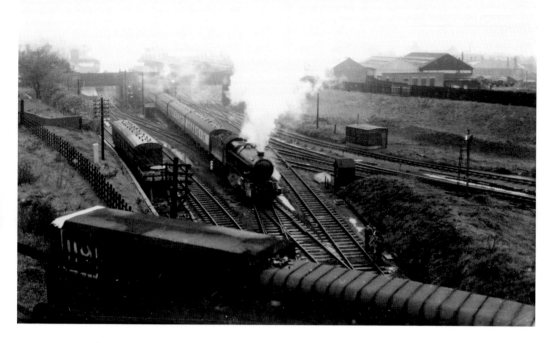

Low Level to Snow Hill

An ex-GWR King Class 4-6-0 heads towards Birmingham Snow Hill with a train for Paddington in the late 1950s having just left Low Level station. The lines to Heath Town Junction are on the right. Below, the transfer of all major services to the newly electrified High Level had its effect on the old GWR station at Wolverhampton as can be seen in this view of a shuttle running between Low Level and Birmingham Snow Hill in 1970.

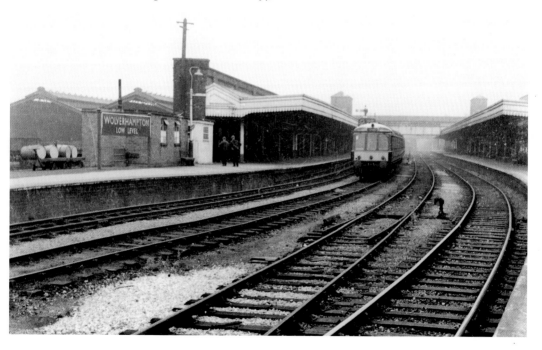

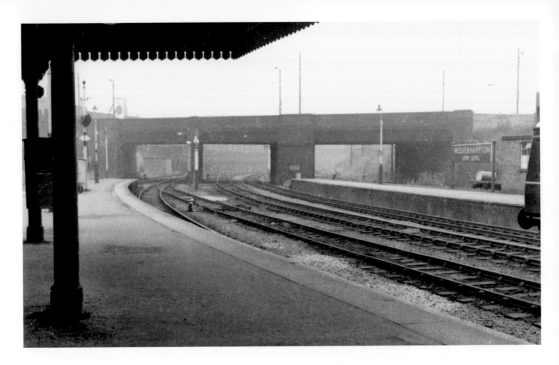

Low Level Station

Above, a final view of Low Level station. The station was used for handling parcels until 1981 and was then closed. It now survives as a Grade II listed building although no trains now run into it. In happier days, a GWR inspection saloon is at Low Level on 20 October 1959. No. 80974 was built at Swindon in 1945 and is now preserved on the North Yorkshire Moors Railway. In the background is Butler's brewery.

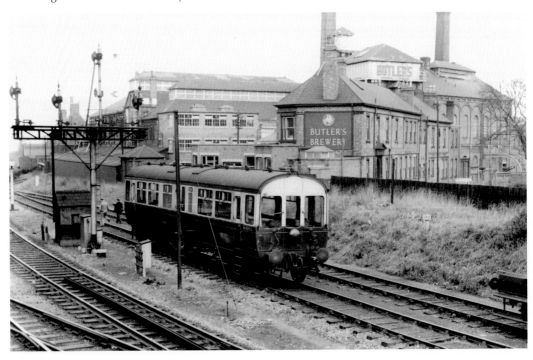

The New Light Railway

The old GWR trackwork from the previous photograph has long disappeared in this 2011 view and even the old Butler's brewery is now being demolished. Below, a new light railway system now links Wolverhampton with the new Snow Hill station using the old BW&D trackbed. Although the old Low Level station is still not used, the tram leaves the old trackbed near to Priestfield. A new terminus is situated close to Wolverhampton town centre at St George. Here, one of the trams is seen at Wolverhampton terminus before it returns to Birmingham.

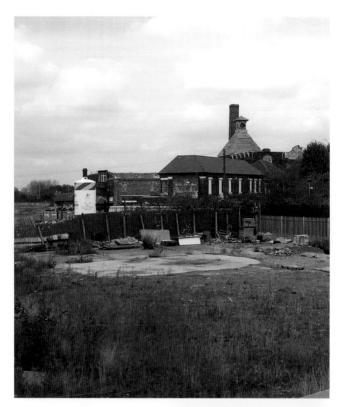

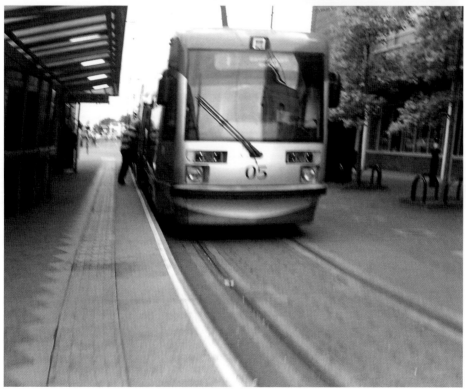

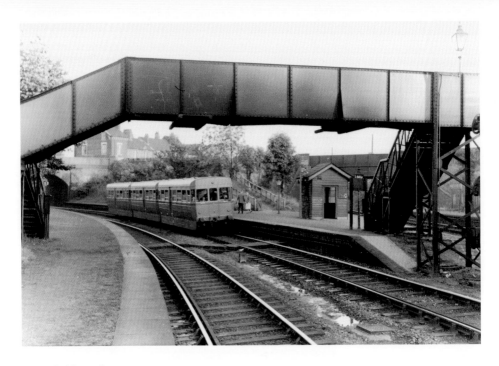

Priestfield Station

Above is the junction station at Priestfield on 18 August 1953 with an experimental diesel unit, built jointly by AEC and Leyland in 1952 *en route* from Snow Hill to Low Level. To the right is the OW&W line to Stourbridge, Worcester and Oxford. Priestfield was the point where the BW&D line met the OW&W for access into Wolverhampton. Below is the first station from Priestfield at Dudley, now sadly disappeared. The station here was jointly owned by the GWR and its old enemy the LNWR, whose South Staffordshire Railway from Walsall joined the OW&W at this point and where the Euston company hoped to thwart the efforts of the GWR to extend its broad gauge beyond Birmingham.

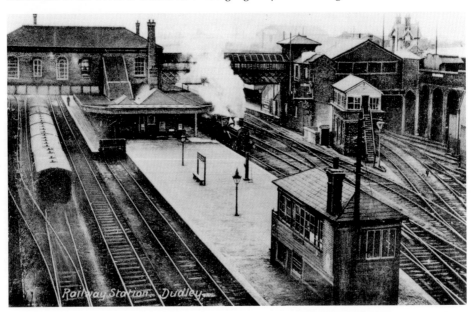

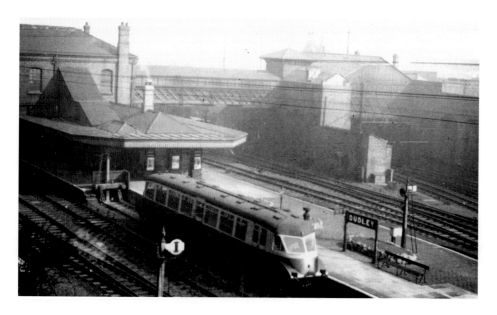

Oxford, Worcester and Wolverhampton Line

A GWR railcar waits at the buffer stops at Dudley station in the 1930s. The Oxford, Worcester & Wolverhampton Railway was to be the first railway to build a line into Dudley and the route was given royal assent on 4 August 1845, despite opposition from the London & Birmingham Railway, whose monopoly in Birmingham could be undermined. The line was to be broad gauge, but disputes with the GWR, who were guarantors, and financial difficulties meant that the line was built to standard gauge after friendly relations with the LNWR developed. There was even agreement that both the LNWR and Midland Railway could operate OW&W trains. It was not until 20 December 1852 that a 6-mile section was opened between Brettel Lane and Stourbridge. Below, the LNWR side of the station can be seen here with a train for Walsall drawing up. As can be seen, the opposite platform is for trains to Birmingham New Street.

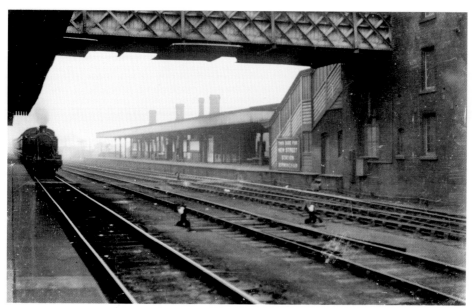

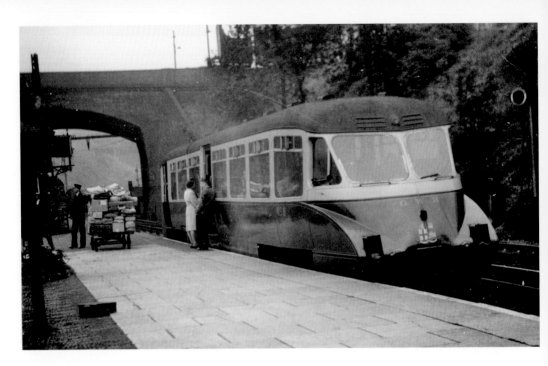

Dudley

A GWR diesel railcar is taking on parcels at Dudley in the 1930s. At this time, both the GWR and LMS were experimenting with diesel traction and further developments may well have taken place but for the intervention of the Second World War. Below is the portal of Dudley Tunnel in 1960.

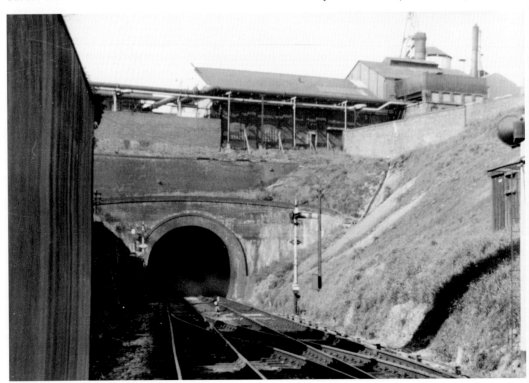

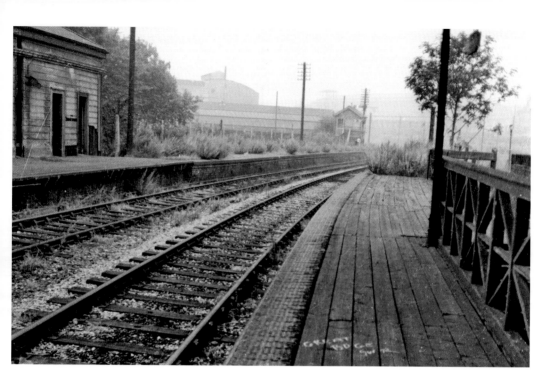

OW&W Stations

Two stations on the OW&W line in the Black Country. Above is Great Bridge, Tipton, while below is Princes End and Coseley. Such were the problems with construction and train services on the OW&W in the early years that it gained the nickname 'Old Worse and Worse', until the GWR assumed ownership and completed works and operated train services.

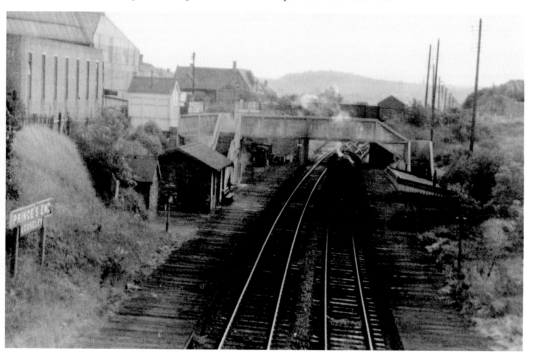

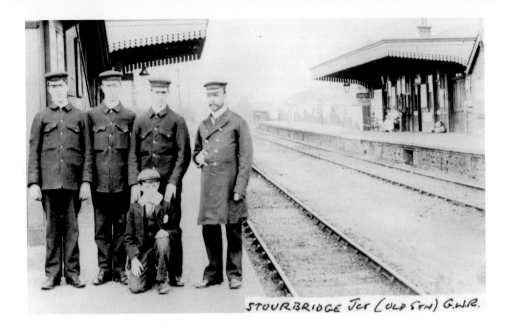

STOURBRIDGE JCT (OLD STN) G.W.R.

Stourbridge Junction Station

Above are station staff at Stourbridge Junction of the OW&W which was closed in 1901. It was between here and Brettel Lane that the first OW&W trains ran. Below, the new GWR Stourbridge Junction station is seen with what appears to be a Dean Goods 0-6-0 at the head of a local train in pre-First World War years. As an important centre of glass production with increasing prosperity, Stourbridge was an attraction for several railway companies. The first to show interest was the Birmingham, Wolverhampton & Stour Valley Railway, promoted by the Shrewsbury & Birmingham Railway in the early 1840s, which would have brought the LNWR into the town. In the end, however, it came to be served by the GWR who had taken control of the OW&W.

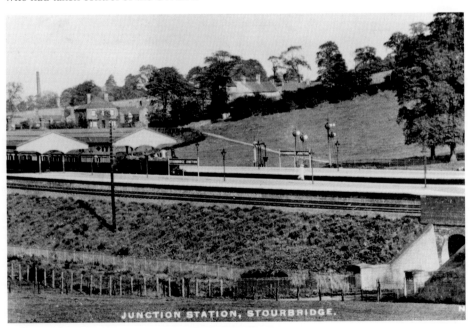

JUNCTION STATION, STOURBRIDGE.

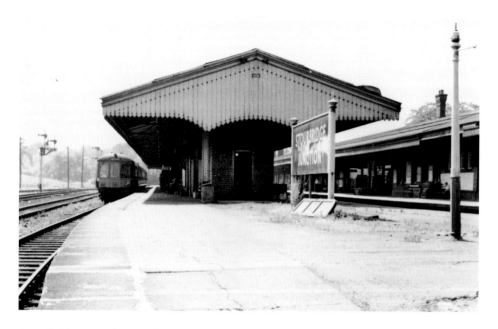

Stourbridge Junction Station

Above is Stourbridge Junction station in the 1960s with a diesel multiple unit calling at the station. Below, the station still remains *in situ* and is well served by Cross-City services, which operate between Stratford-upon-Avon, Whitlocks End, Birmingham Snow Hill, Stourbridge Junction and Worcester. Here a new Class 172 DMU has brought in a train from Stratford-upon-Avon and will go forward to Worcester Foregate Street, while a Class 150 Sprinter is about to depart for Whitlocks End, in September 2011.

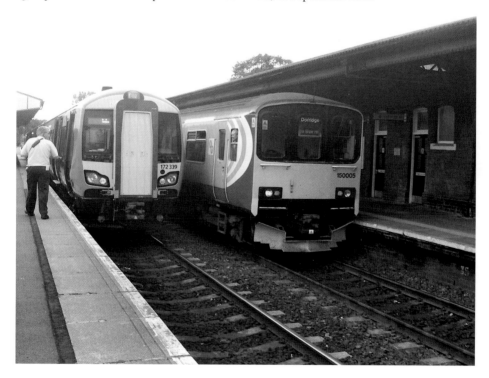

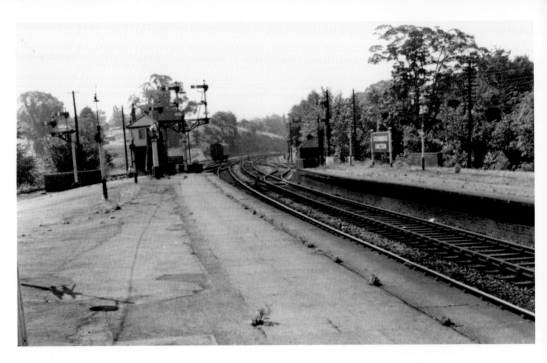

Stourbridge Junction station
The Birmingham end of Stourbridge Junction station in the 1960s and in September 2011.

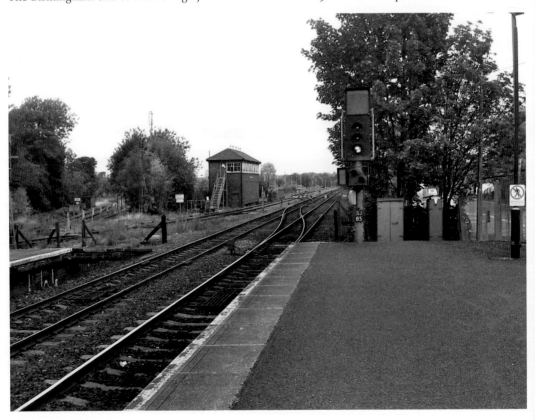

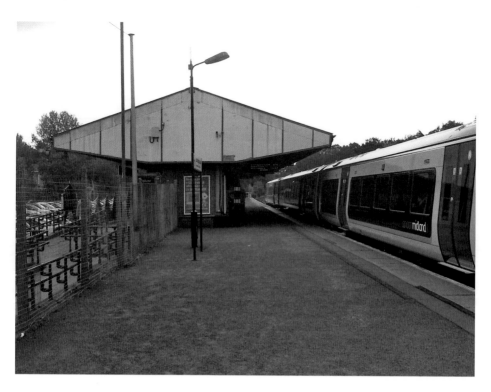

Stourbridge Junction Station

Above, a Worcester-bound train waits at Stourbridge Junction in 2011. Below, the car park and station nameboard in the same year.

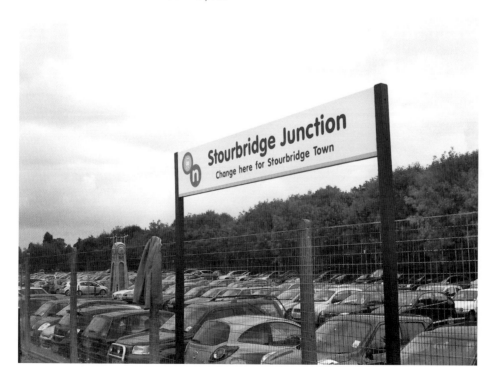

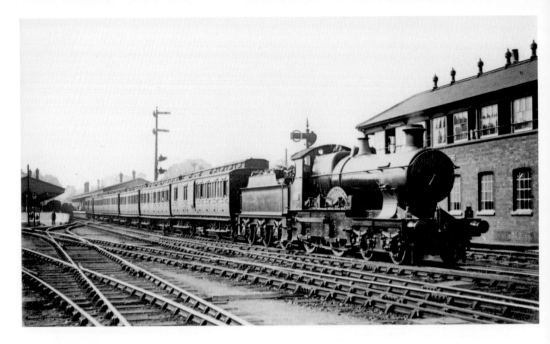

Stourbridge Junction
Above, GWR double-framed Dean 4-4-0 No. 3444 heads an express made up of red GWR coaches through Stourbridge Junction on its way from Worcester to Wolverhampton Low Level in the years prior to the First World War. Below, Stourbridge Junction in 2011 showing the single line branch to Stourbridge Town station.

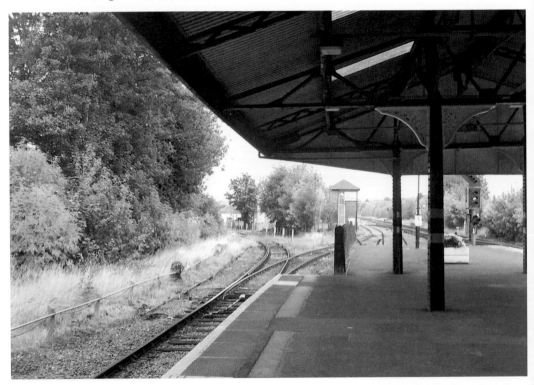

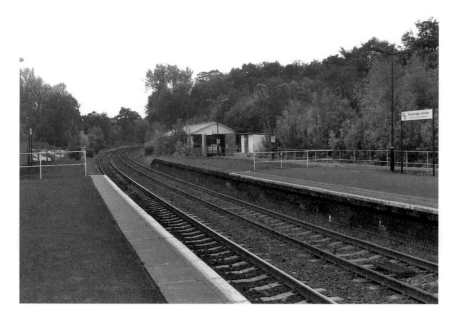

Stourbridge Shuttle Service

The end of the little branch at Stourbridge Junction with the engine shed, which houses the shuttle, that runs between the junction and Stourbridge Town station. Below, the shuttle runs into Stourbridge Junction station with its ten-minute service from Stourbridge Town station. In steam days, the shuttle was operated by a GWR railmotor with an 0-6-0 pannier tank providing motive power. In BR days, these railmotors were named after birds and *Wren* was often seen on this shuttle service. Diesel units took over from steam at its demise and the little shuttle today is powered by liquid petroleum gas and can carry as many as seventy passengers at its busiest times.

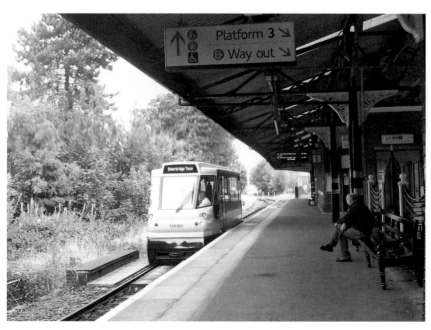

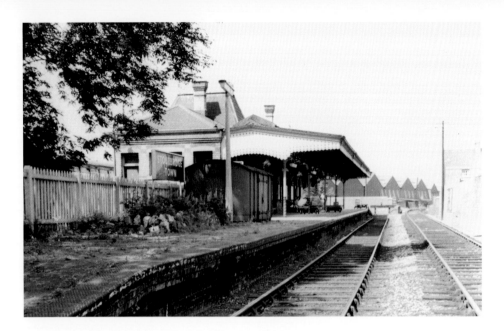

Stourbridge Town Station

Above is Stourbridge Town station in the 1950s. The town centre lies about a mile away from the junction and, in 1865, the Stourbridge Railway obtained an Act to construct a branch from the junction, but these powers lapsed before construction could begin. The GWR acquired a fresh Act in 1874 but five years elapsed before the branch was completed. Just beyond the station, goods facilities were provided at Stourbridge Basin. Below is the modern station sign for Stourbridge Town.

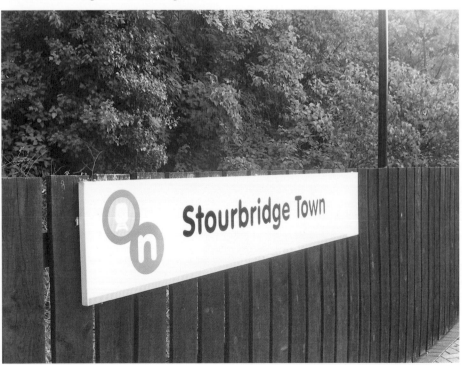

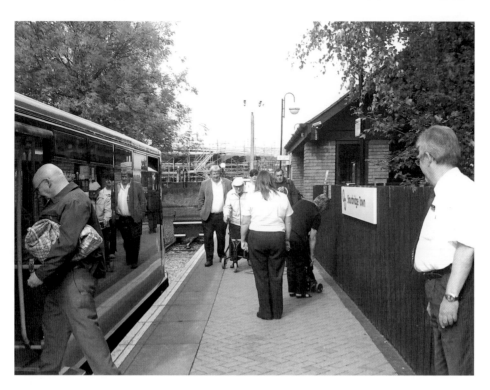

Stourbridge Town Station
Stourbridge Town station and the shuttle unit in September 2011; the station still remains busy at this time.

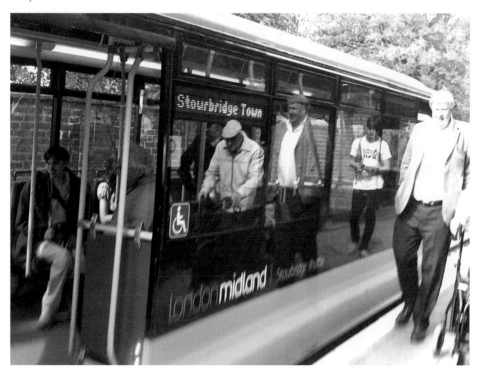

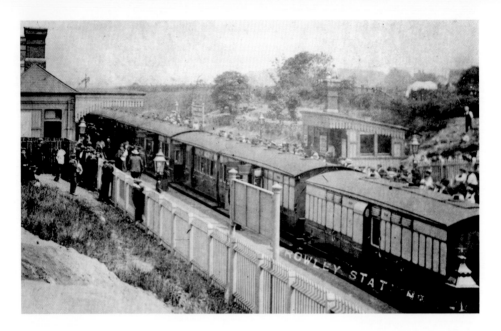

Rowley Regis

Along with the line from Wolverhampton, Stourbridge also was the junction for a line from Birmingham Snow Hill, via Smethwick to Kidderminster and Worcester. That line is still in use from the new Snow Hill station and running parallel to the new tramway as far as The Hawthorns and then branches off. From Stourbridge, one of the stations is Rowley Regis, seen here during the First World War with soldiers about to leave for the Western Front. Below is the modern Rowley Regis station in 2011.

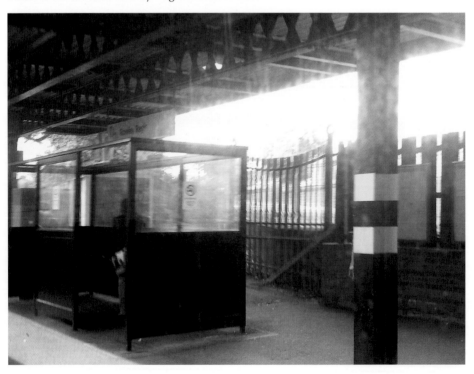

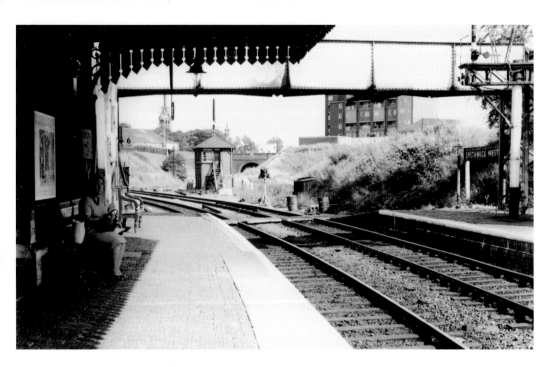

Handsworth & Smethwick Station
Before approaching the junction with the BW&D lay Smethwick Junction, seen here in the 1950s. Below is the BW&D station of Handsworth & Smethwick. The little Black Country town has been well served by the railways for many years and several stations have existed here since the early railway days.

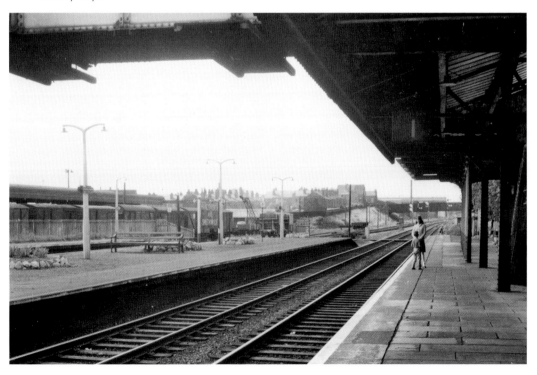

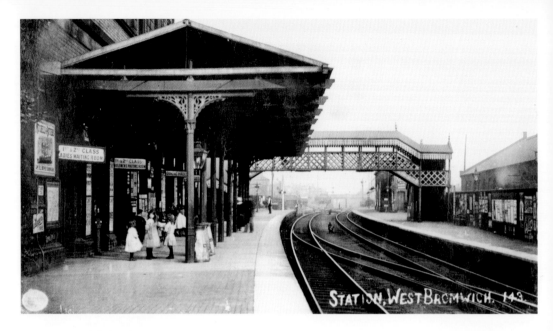

West Bromwich Station

West Bromwich station on the BW&D line in the late nineteenth century. The BW&D ran from Birmingham Snow Hill to Priestfield, where it met the OW&W for access to Low Level. It was authorised in 1846, but work was not commenced until 1851 as the GWR had entered into futile negotiations with the LNWR to share their Stour Valley line from Birmingham New Street to High Level. The Euston company was doing all they possibly could to stop the GWR ever reaching Wolverhampton. In the end, the GWR merged with the standard-gauge S&B and the BW&D was built as a mixed-gauge line, due to the belligerence of the LNWR in stopping the S&B using the Stour Valley line in order to stop the GWR having access to it. Below is the important BW&D station at Wednesbury.

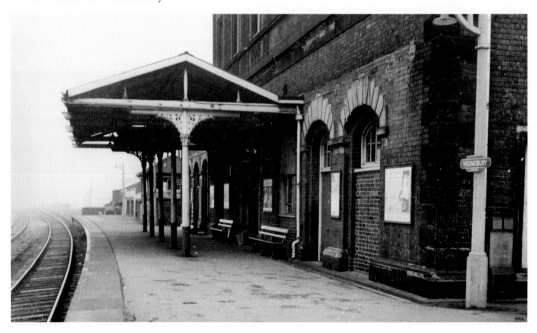

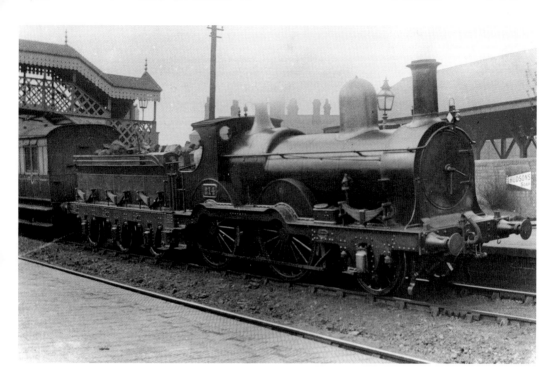

GWR

Above is an Armstrong 2-4-0 GWR loco. No. 214 on a local train at Wednesbury in 1903. The engine was built locally at Wolverhampton's Stafford Road Locomotive works, which had been building engines for the Northern Division of the GWR from 1854. The works continued to build engines for the GWR until all such work was transferred to Swindon in 1908. Below, is the GWR station of Bilston Central in the 1950s.

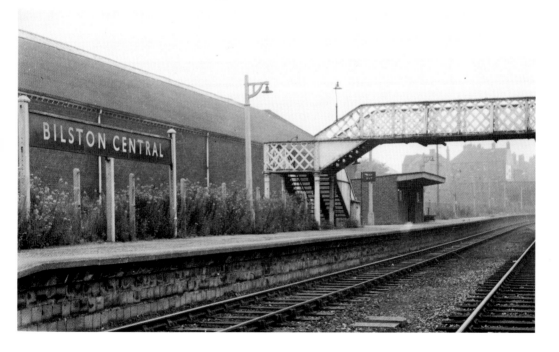

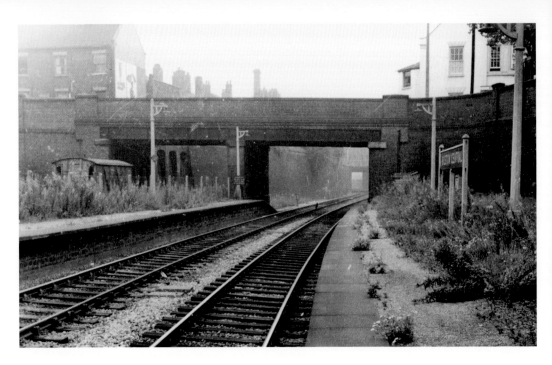

Bilston Central
Two views of Bilston Central. The upper view shows the station in the 1950s, while the lower picture is of the station on the new tramway system in 2011.

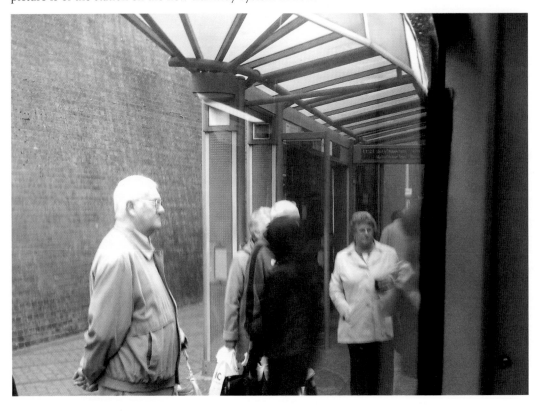

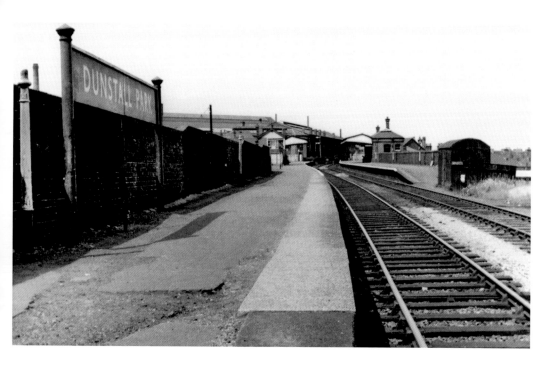

Dunstall Park Station

Dunstall Park station on the Wolverhampton Junction Railway which brought the S&B into Low Level station. The GWR opened Dunstall Park as an intermediate station on 1 December 1896 and it would later assume an important role dealing with railway traffic serving the nearby racecourse. The station also lay close to the Stafford Road works, which can be seen nestling against the platform in the lower view.

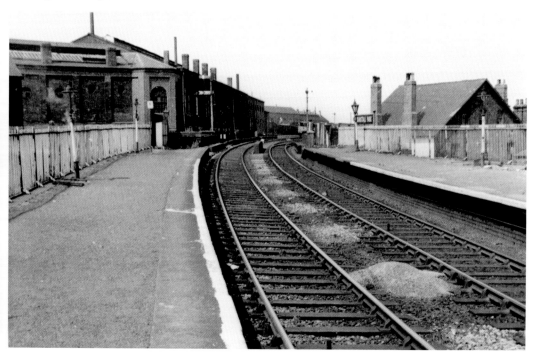

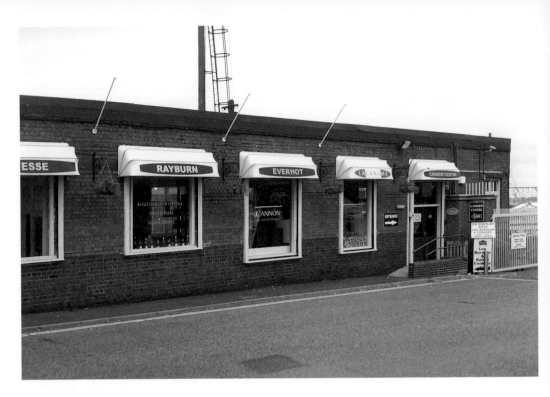

Dunstall Park Station

The upper view shows the main building of the old Dunstall Park station in 2011, now in use as offices for a local builders' merchant, its main warehouse being situated in the old locoworks. Below, back in 1956, a Talyllyn special train to the narrow-gauge railway passes Oxley Middle Junction as it approaches the S&B line from Shrewsbury. The left-hand line is the Wombourn branch.

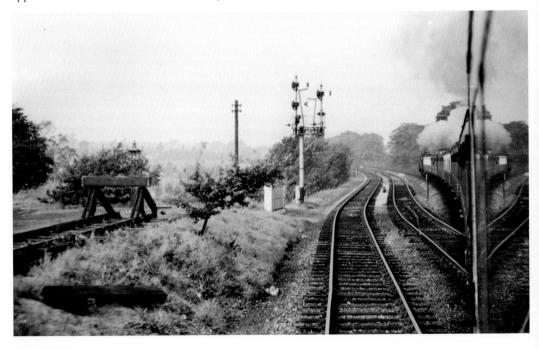

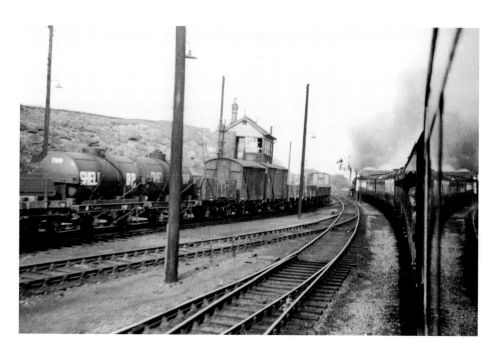

Talyllyn Special

Another view of the Talyllyn special passing Oxley in 1956, with ex-MR three-cylinder compound No. 41123 at the head. Oxley sidings are on the left with various wagons in the siding and Oxley North signal box is also in view. Below is the station approach at Albrighton on the S&B line to Shrewsbury. Although the S&B was instrumental in the development of High Level station and the construction of the Stour Valley line from New Street, it fell into the hands of the GWR after its line had been opened in 1849. The LNWR refused to allow the Shrewsbury company access to its station and caused a riot when the little company wanted to use the canal basin there. The LNWR even refused to open the Stour Valley line in an effort to prevent GWR access.

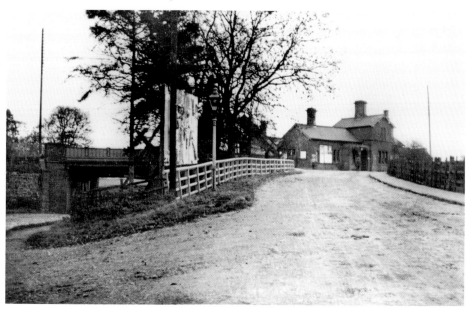

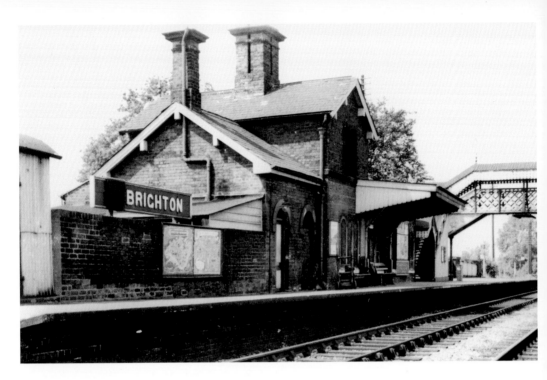

Albrighton Station

Another view of Albrighton station in the 1960s, while below is Wombourn station on the Wombourn branch, opened in 1925. The branch ran between Oxley and Brettel Lane and was 12 miles long with a passing loop at Wombourn. Steam railmotors operated services along the branch but there were few passengers and such services ceased on 31 October 1932.

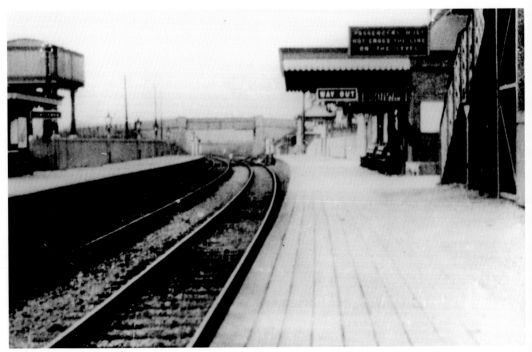

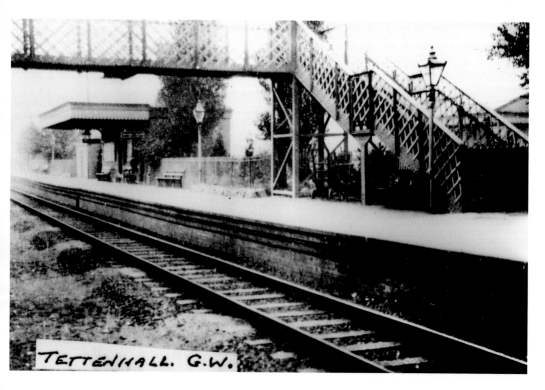

TETTENHALL. G.W.

Tettenhall Station

Two views of Tettenhall station on the Wombourn branch. The upper view shows the station not long after opening, while the lower picture shows the station on 19 September 1965, shortly after the line had finally been closed.

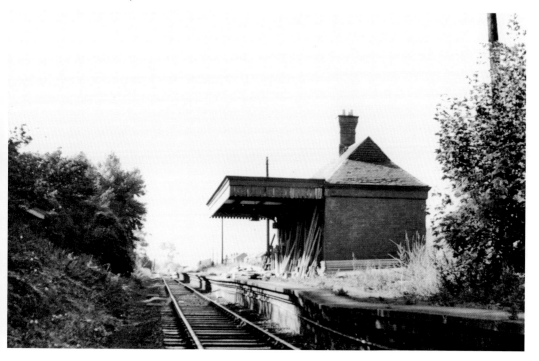

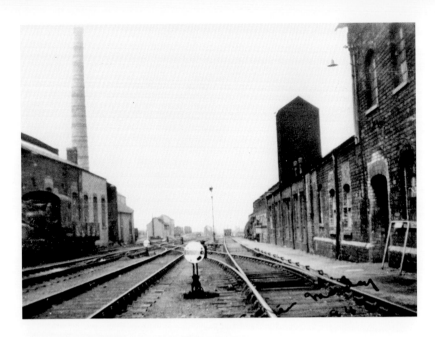

Stafford Road Locomotive Works

Two views of the exterior of the Stafford Road Locomotive Works, Wolverhampton. Workshops were originally established here by the S&B in 1849 with limited facilities, as the Shrewsbury company's line was worked by contract, although the company did own the engines used and only repair work was undertaken. The works virtually ceased to exist when the Wolverhampton Junction Railway was built. The S&B and Shrewsbury and Chester were absorbed into the GWR in 1854 and its Northern Division was set up then. It was S&B Engineer, Joseph Armstrong, who decided to establish a locoworks here and engines continued to be built here until 1908, after which the works was responsible for heavy maintenance work on GWR locos operating in the area. The works continued to maintain engines until closure in June 1964.

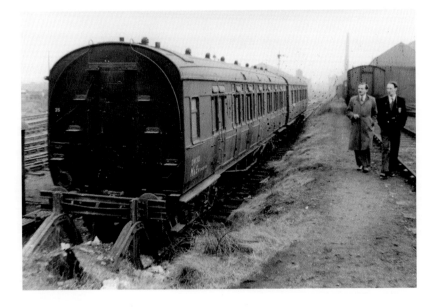

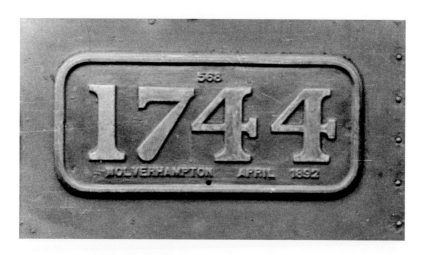

Stafford Road Locomotive Works

Above is a numberplate for GWR o-6-o Pannier Tank No. 1744 which was built at Wolverhampton in 1892, as a saddle tank, seen at Croes Newydd shed, Wrexham, on 6 August 1935. Below is the erecting shop at the Stafford Road works. This new shop was built in the 1930s along with a machine shop and wheel shop. The site was rather cramped, being situated between the GWR and LMS lines. Through all of the years that GWR steam engines existed, they all carried one feature, which was established at Wolverhampton; the famous brass safety valve bonnet was originally designed at the works as an apprentice piece. Thus, although the works ceased to build engines, its legacy remained on every GWR engine built.

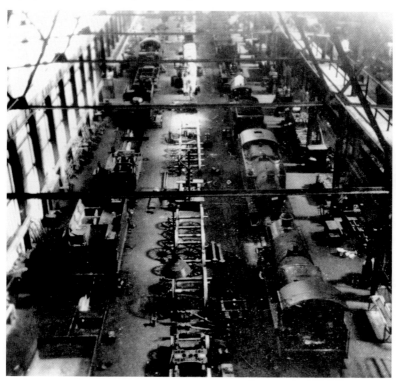

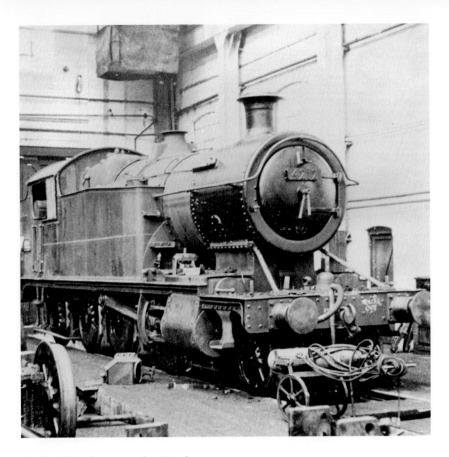

Stafford Road Locomotive Works

Locomotives under repair at the works. The upper view shows Churchward 2-8-0T No. 4212 in the 1950s and the lower shows 0-6-0PT No. 3740, of the 8750 class, undergoing heavy overhaul on 7 May 1950. At its peak, the works employed some 1,500 men and was an important part of the local economy.

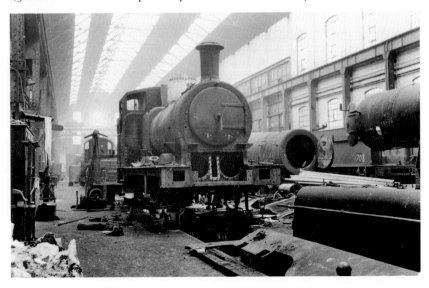

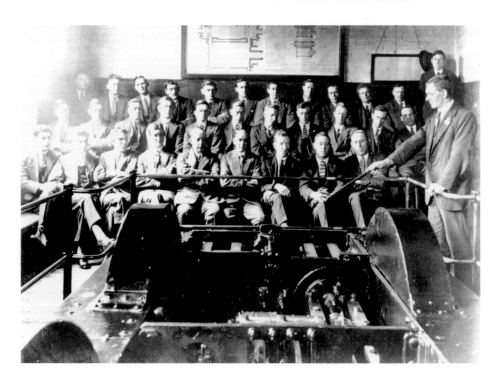

Stafford Road Locomotive Works

The upper view shows engine men being educated on the workings of GWR engines at the Stafford Road works. The engine used for the lesson is ex-West Midland Railway 0-6-0 built by E. B. Wilson & Co. of Leeds in 1855. Its WMR (and OW&W) number was 34 and its GWR number was 252. The loco. was withdrawn in August 1904. Below, staff pose next to GWR Churchward four-cylinder star class 4-6-0 No. 4067 *Tintern Abbey* at around 1923 shortly after the engine had been built at Swindon. The loco. retained its inside steam pipes throughout its life and was withdrawn in September 1940 and rebuilt as Castle No. 5087, retaining its *Abbey* name.

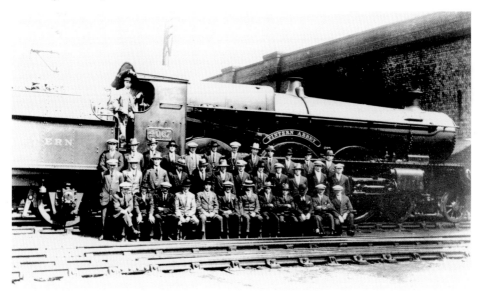

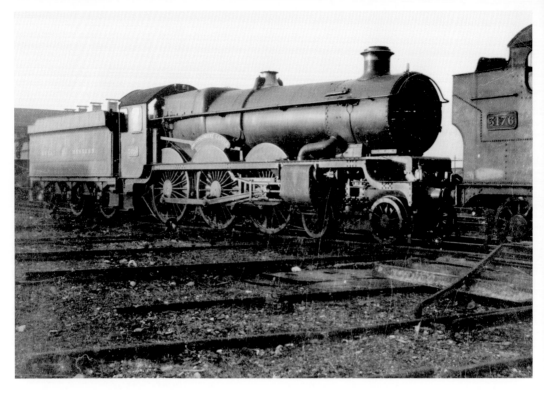

Stafford Road Locomotive Works

Standing outside the works in the 1930s is GWR Collett Castle No. 5016 *Montgomery Castle* with full Great Western livery and crest on the tender. Below, in 1949, are ex-LNWR 0-6-0s outside the works with a GWR Hall 4-6-0 as company.

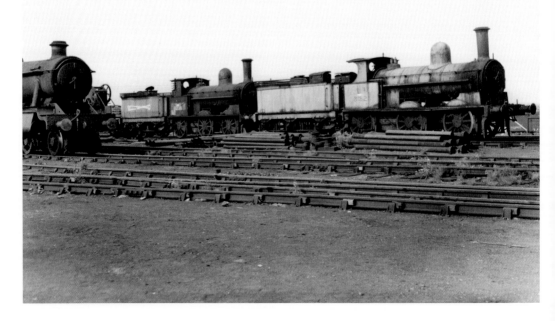

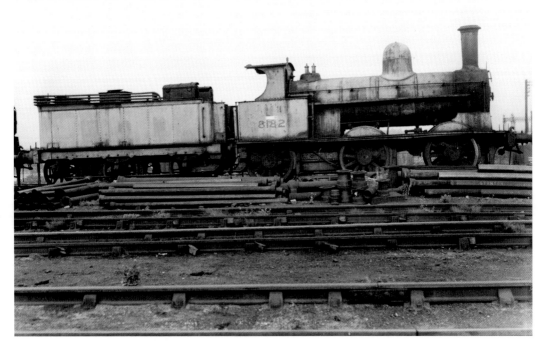

War Department Stock at Stafford Road
Ex-LNWR engines, as War Department stock, at the Stafford Road works on 4 September 1949. The loco. at the top is No. 8182, while the lower view shows No. 8108.

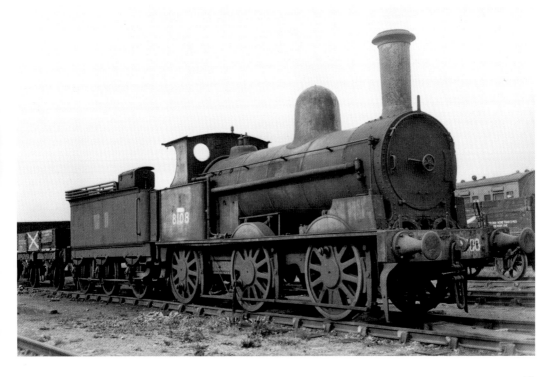

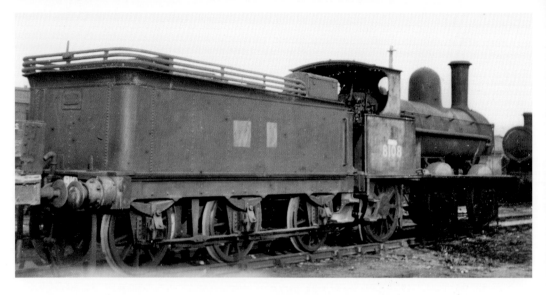

Ex-LNWR 0-6-0 No. 8108
Two views of ex-LNWR 0-6-0 No. 8108 in a poor state of repair.

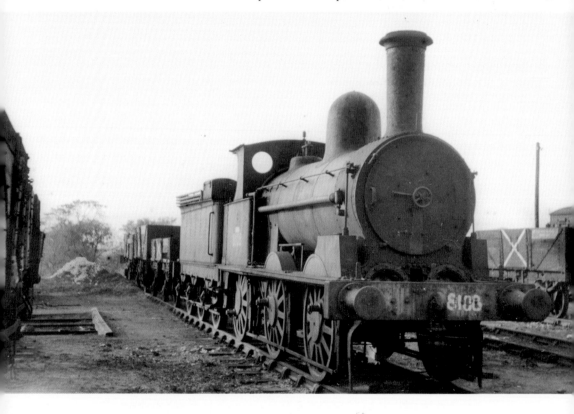

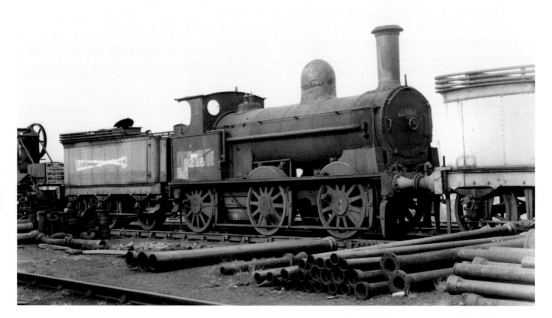

Stafford Road Locomotive Works
The upper view shows another ex-LNWR 0-6-0, No. 8236 awaiting her fate at the works. Below is the last locomotive to be repaired at the Stafford Road works before closure in June 1964. The engine was ex-GWR Churchward 2-8-0 No. 2859, which was allocated to Pontypool Road, South Wales, for operating heavy coal trains from local coalfields. The engine was outshopped in February 1964, as the sign at the front of the engine indicates, four months before the works were finally closed ending 115 years of loco. construction and maintenance in Wolverhampton.

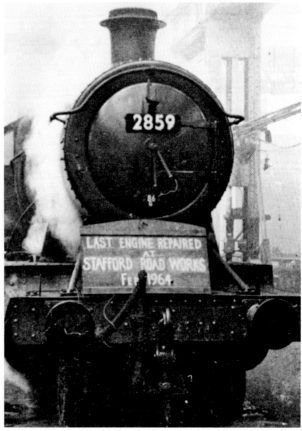

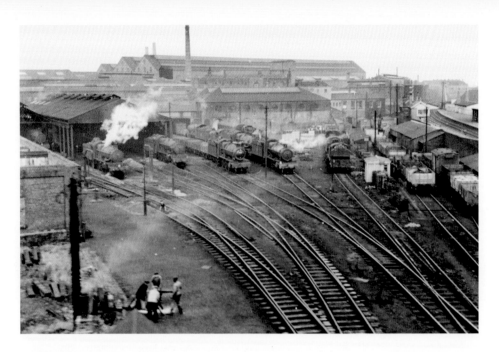

Stafford Road Engine Shed

A panoramic view of the Stafford Road engine shed, with Dunstall Park station on the right and the Stafford Road works behind. A locoshed was established here in 1854 opposite one belonging to the S&B. When there was no hope of the GWR broad gauge ever going any further north than Wolverhampton, the standard-gauge S&B shed was merged with that of the GWR as they converted to the standard gauge. A new shed was opened in 1860 with further additions in 1875. In this panoramic view, there are Hall and Castle Class 4-6-0s along with various tank engines. Below, at the Stafford Road shed in 1931 is double-framed Dean Goods 0-6-0 No. 1195.

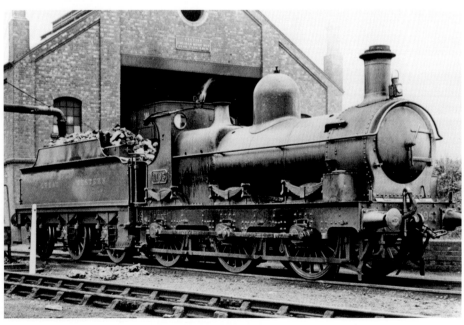

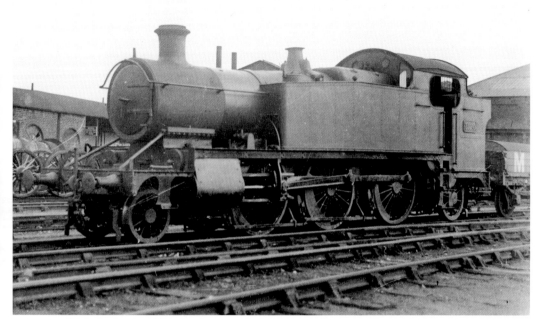

Stafford Road Engine Shed

Outside Stafford Road shed is GWR Churchward 2-6-2 Prairie Tank No. 3120 in the mid-1920s. A loco. boiler and a set of locomotive driving wheels can be seen in the background. Below, is GWR Churchward 2-6-0 No. 5317 with an unidentified 2-8-2T behind.

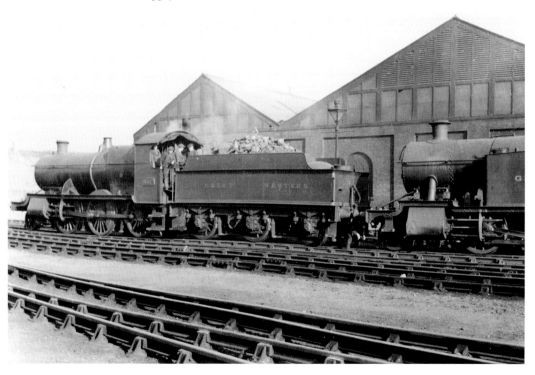

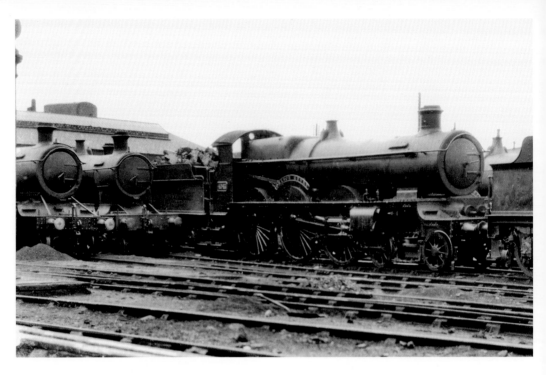

Prince Henry and ***Princess Elizabeth***

The Stafford Road shed around 1935 with Star 4-6-0 No. 4043 *Prince Henry*, a Bulldog 4-4-0 next to her and a 2-6-2T next to that, above. Below, is GWR Churchward 4-6-0 Star No. 4057 *Princess Elizabeth*, which was built in July 1914 and withdrawn in October 1957, outside the shed in 1935.

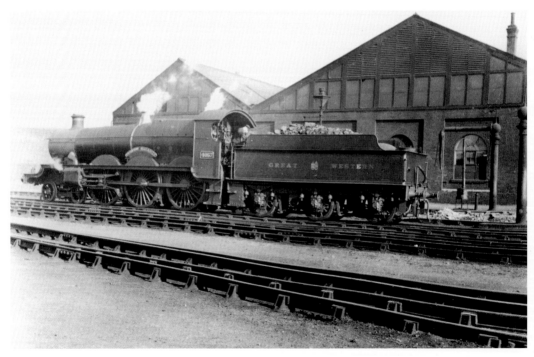

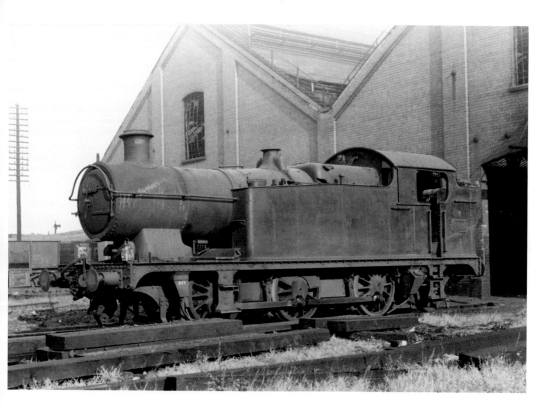

Stafford Road Engine Shed

On 4 September 1949 is 0-6-2T No. 6640 above, while, on the same day Prairie Tank No. 3160 is
hauling coal wagons past Stafford Road shed.

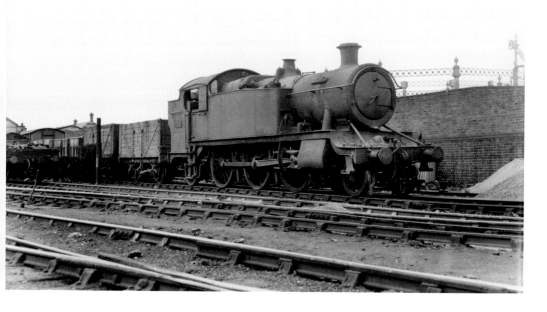

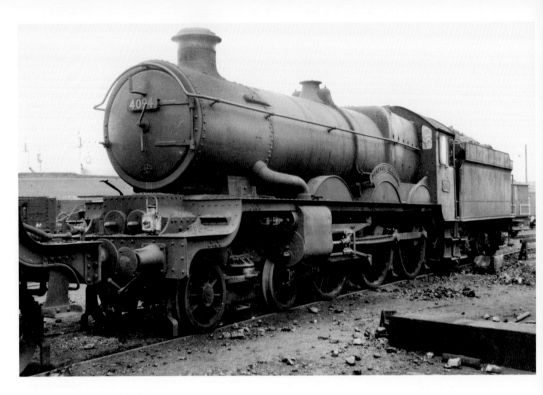

Dynevor Castle and **St Martin**

In the 1950s ex-GWR Castle Class 4-6-0 No. 4094 *Dynevor Castle* is at rest in the yard at Stafford Road and Hall 4-6-0 the famous *Saint Martin*, rebuilt from the doyen of the Churchward Class two-cylinder 4-6-0 of 1902, is at the coaling stage. The engine was scrapped in 1959.

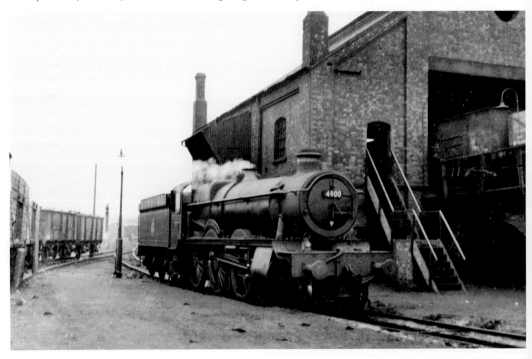

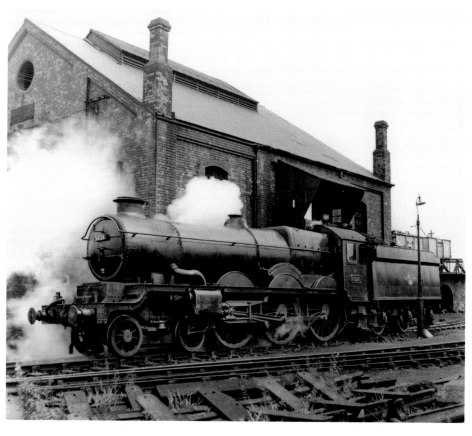

Criccieth Castle

Above is another Castle 4-6-0 No. 5026 *Criccieth Castle,* with double chimney, at the coaling stage in 1959. Below, in the same period, is Churchward 2-6-0 No. 5300.

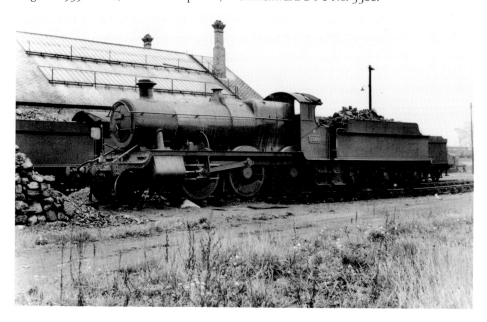

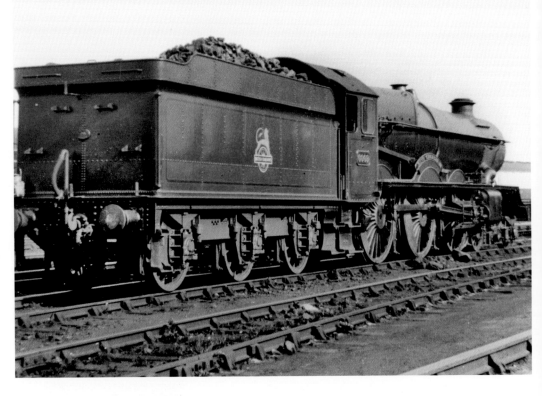

King Charles II and **Powis Castle**
The above view shows ex-GWR King Class 4-6-0 No. 6009 *King Charles II* at Stafford Road shed in 1955. Below, a year later is Castle No. 7024 *Powis Castle*, one of a few built by BR in 1950.

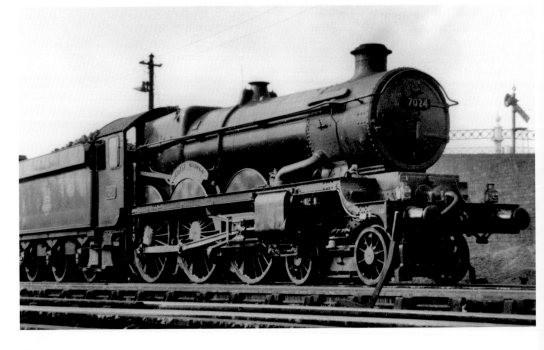

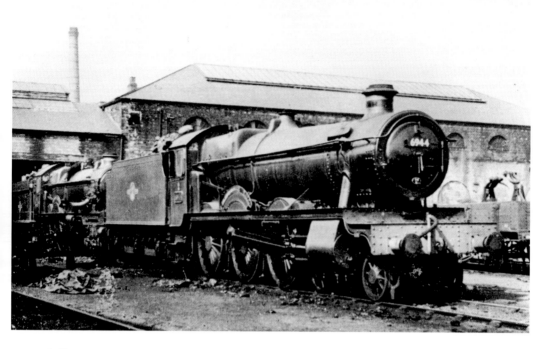

Fledborough Hall and *Earl of Powis*

At Stafford Road shed in the late 1950s is Hawksworth Modified Hall No. 6944 *Fledborough Hall*, with flat-sided tender and an unidentified Castle behind. Below is 5056 *Earl of Powis* with 0-6-0 Pannier Tank No. 4683 next to it.

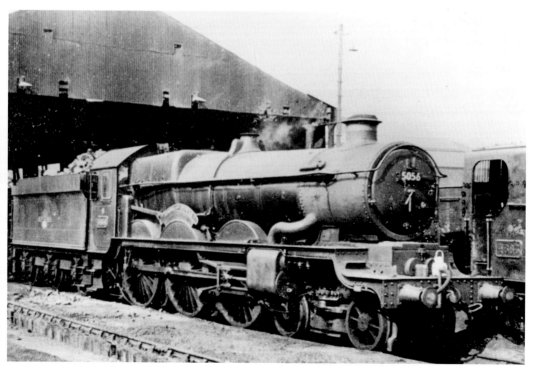

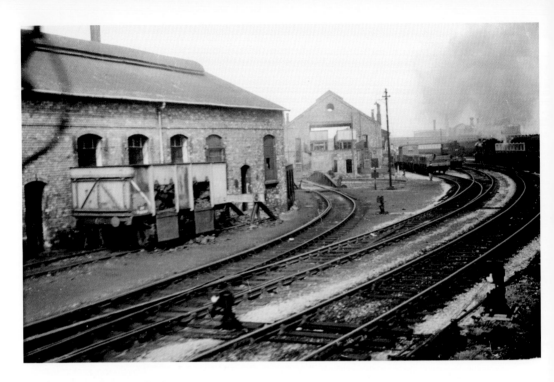

Stafford Road Engine Shed

Ex-MR three-cylinder Compound 4-4-0 No. 41123 heads a train past the coaling stage at Stafford Road shed in 1956. A pannier tank can be seen shunting in the background. Below, a three-car DMU is passing Stafford Road shed on the Wolverhampton Junction Railway, 13 June 1957.

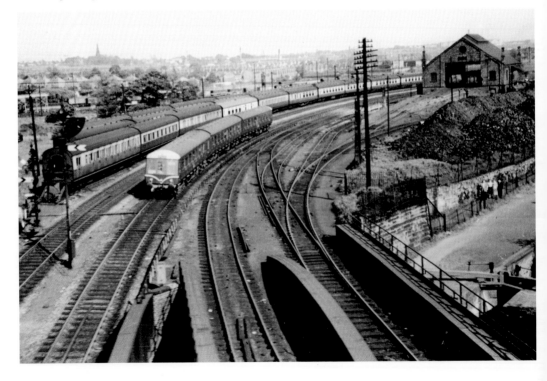

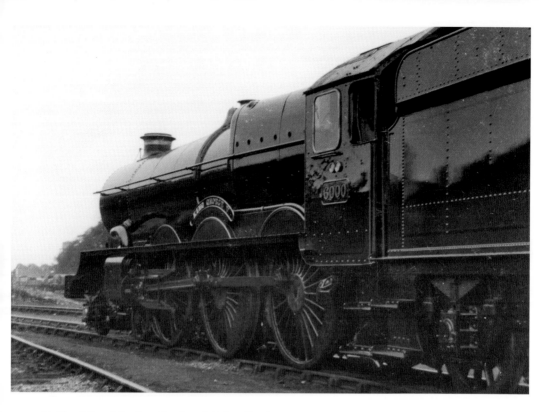

Stafford Road Engine Shed and Oxley Shed
Above, Stafford Road shed in 1956 with doyen of the GWR King Class No. 6000 *King George V.*
Below, standing outside Oxley shed is ex-GWR Grange Class 4-6-0 No. 6839 *Hewell Grange.*

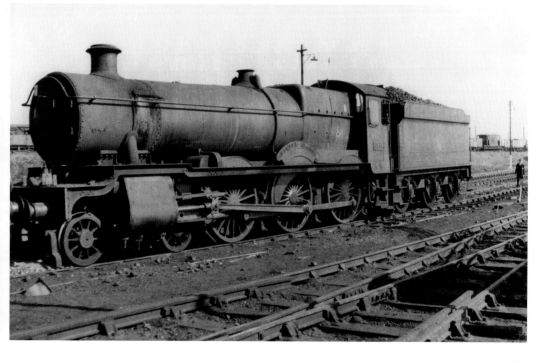

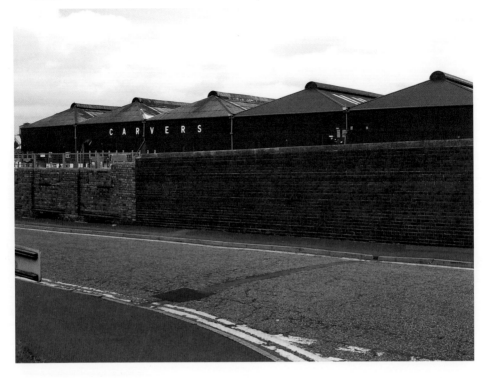

Closure of Stafford Road

The Stafford Road shed was closed in 1963 and the buildings are now used as a warehouse for a builders' merchants, as can be seen in these 2011 views.

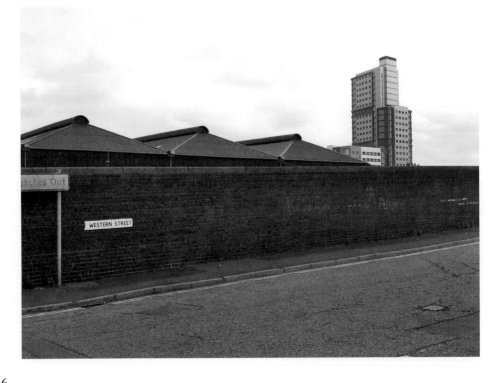

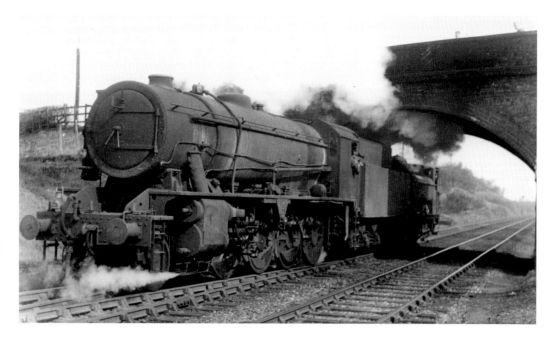

Oxley Engine Shed

Ex WD 2-8-0 No. 77165 in company with an 0-6-0 pannier tank head towards Oxley on 13 April 1947. While below, GWR 0-6-0 Dean Goods 0-6-0 sits in Oxley shed on 4 September 1949. Oxley shed was opened in 1907 to relieve pressure on Stafford Road and was situated close to the racecourse. It was 25 feet above natural ground and was built on arches. Its role was to provide motive power for freight work. It lasted until March 1967, supplying engines for Wolverhampton's needs after Stafford Road was closed.

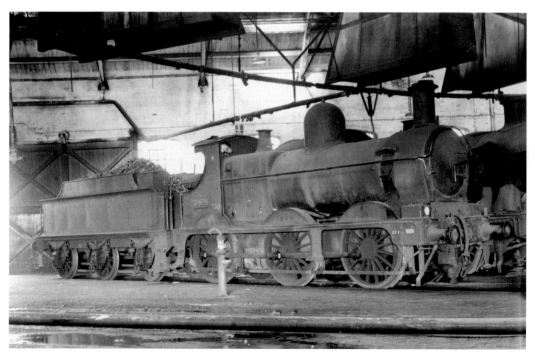

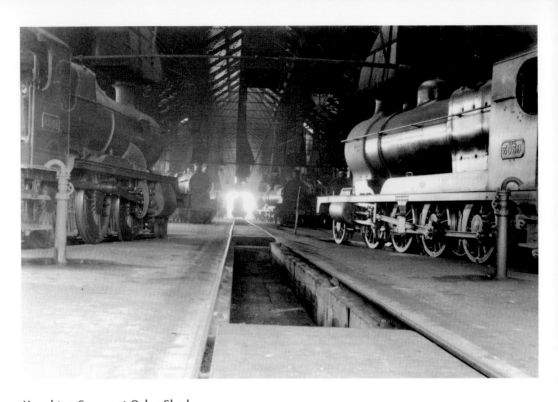

Haughton Grange at Oxley Shed

Above is the interior of Oxley shed in 1935 with ex-ROD 2-8-0 of GCR design No. 3039 and Churchward 2-6-0 No. 8341 at rest. Below is ex-GWR Grange Class 4-6-0 No. 6874 *Haughton Grange* with 3500-gallon Collett tender, at the coaling stage of Oxley shed in 1958.

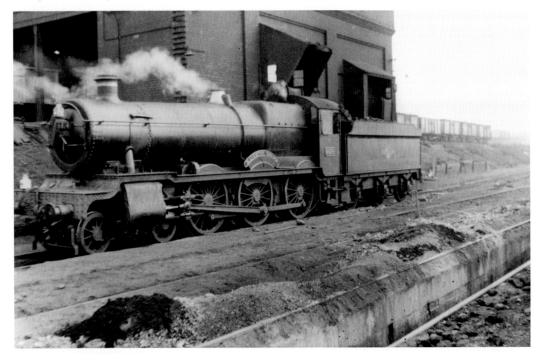

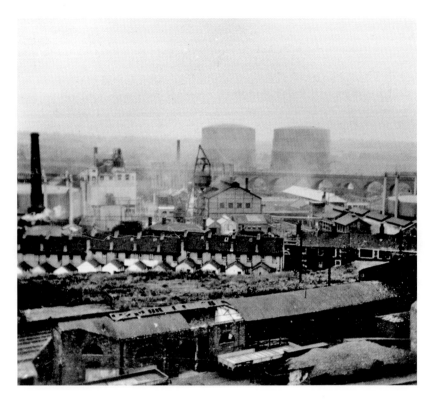

LNWR Viaduct

Above is a view of the LNWR viaduct which the line to Bushbury, with the gasworks in front along with the GWR lines to Low Level and Herbert Street goods depot. The terraced houses are in Stafford Road close to the GWR works. Nowadays, the town is very different although viaduct remains, as this 2011 view shows.

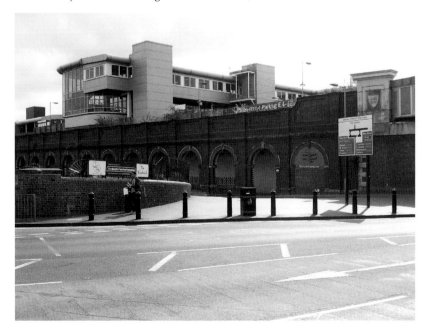

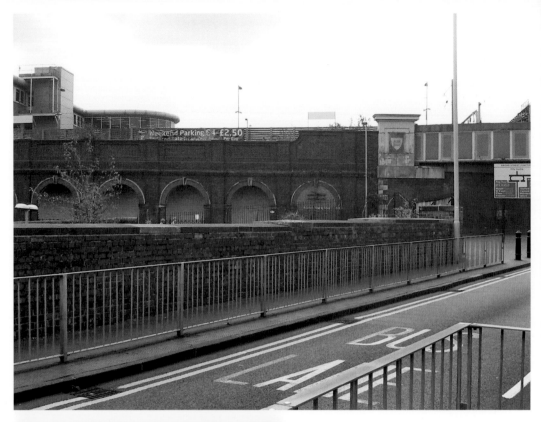

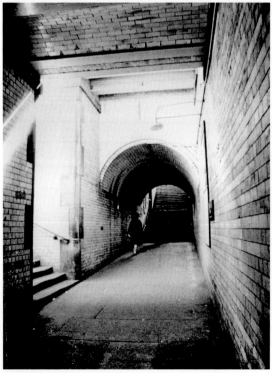

LNWR Viaduct

Another view of the LNWR viaduct at Wolverhampton station in 2011. Below, both stations were open, when a tunnel linked them. The low level entrance to the tunnel can be seen on the left. In its early days, this tunnel was known as 'The Brothel' because of the nightly occurrences there.

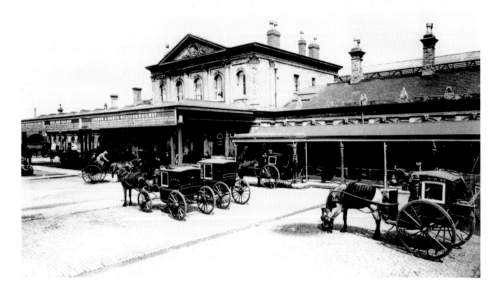

High Level Station

The upper view shows Wolverhampton High Level station in 1907 with its array of hansom cabs awaiting their turn of duty. This exterior view shows that it was jointly used by the LNWR, whose Stour Valley line ran in from Birmingham New Street, and the Midland Railway, who had a line from Walsall. At the far end, there is a sign which directs passengers down the infamous tunnel to Low Level. Land for the station was purchased by the S&B in 1847 and the company's architect, Edward Banks, designed the station. The station opened under LNWR auspices, thanks to disputes with the S&B in 1852 and was originally called Wolverhampton General, but later became Queen Street. Following electrification in the 1960s, the station was rebuilt by British Railways in March 1967. The new, concrete structure is visible here. Many improvements have been carried out over the years as it is now the only main line station to serve the town.

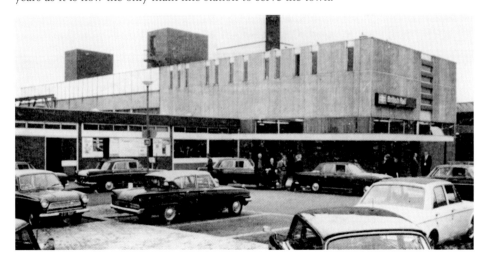

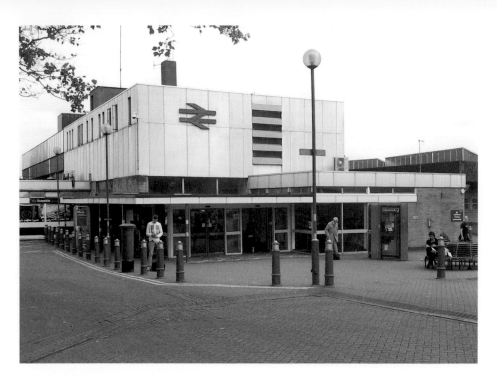

High Level Station

The exterior of High Level station in 2011. Most of the original 1960s structure is still in use. There is, also an interchange here with local bus services. The main bus station can be seen in the lower view.

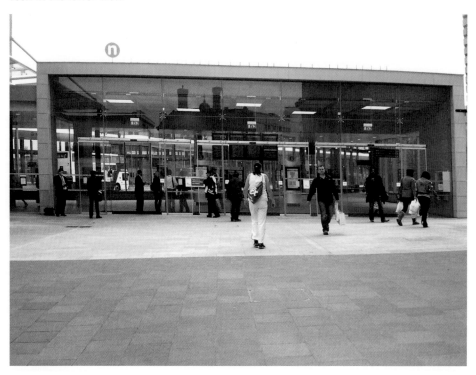

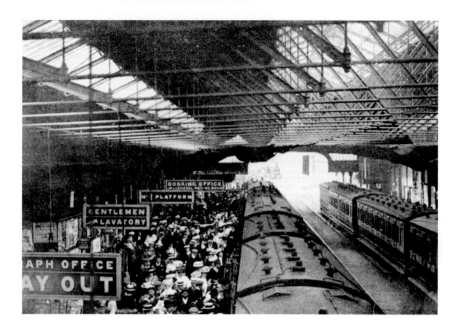

Queen Street Station

The packed interior of Queen Street station in 1908. The station always suffered from insufficient accommodation and the LNWR proposed to extend the station. Unfortunately, these plans encroached on to the public road to Low Level and the GWR opposed the scheme (as they would, given the enmity between the two companies). The town council also devised improvement schemes that involved diversion of the approach road away from the arched entrance to a junction with the 1883-built Lichfield Street. As a result of these opposing plans, and objections, work on station improvements did not begin until 1884. The reconstructed station remained in use until rebuilding in the early 1960s.

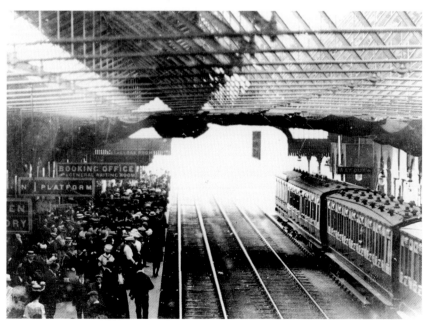

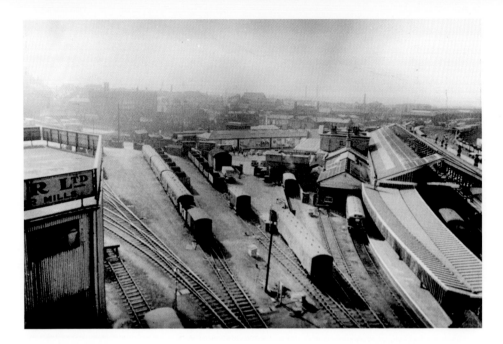

High Level Station

The upper view shows High Level station in June 1960 with a DMU on a local service and a diesel-electric loco. on a Birmingham-bound express. Mill Street goods depot is on the left and the cattle dock is out of view further to the left. The picture was probably taken from the goods shed roof. The lower view shows an unidentified Stanier Black Five 4-6-0 at the head of a train for Birmingham in 1960. In view are the goods avoiding lines at High Level, the frontage of the GWK Low Level station with a pannier tank on shunting duties, and the GWR carriage shed.

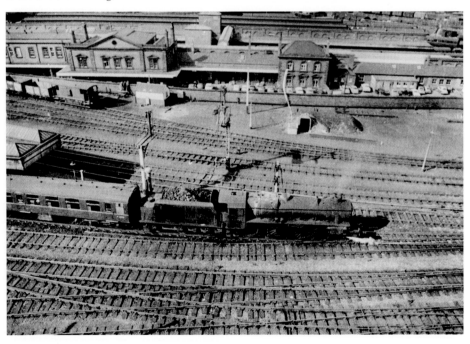

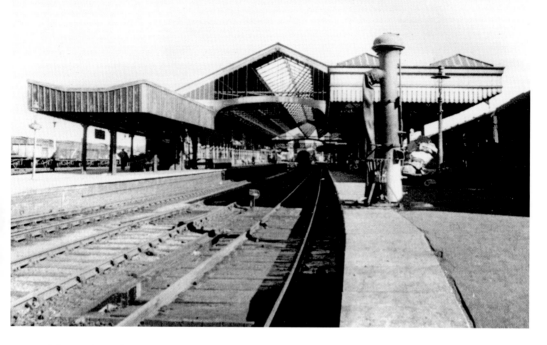

High Level Station

The northern end of High Level station in 1960 with goods siding off to the left. The overall roof looks somewhat worse for wear and the general state of the station brought many complaints. The station was still lit by gas until the 1960s rebuild. The lower view shows a Birmingham-bound train in the distance and a pile of mail bags.

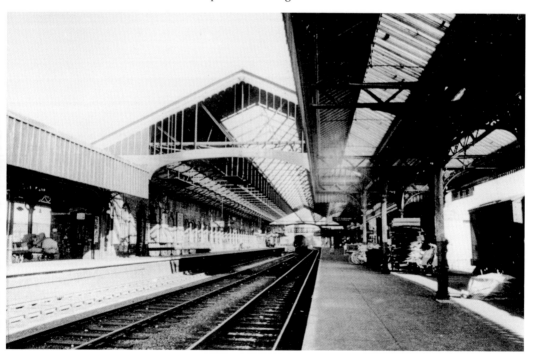

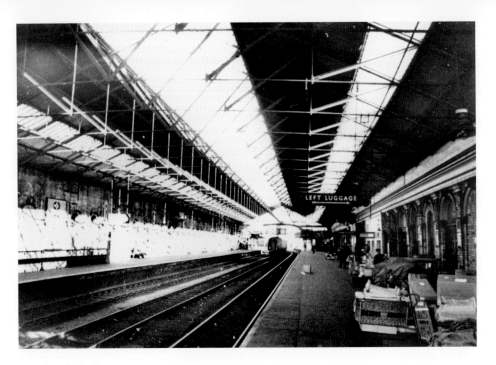

High Level Station

Above is the heart of High Level station in 1960 with a Birmingham-bound train in the distance and piles of parcels, mailbags, and pigeon baskets. Below is the south end of the station with the goods wagons of Mill Street goods depot on the right with ex-LMS Class 3F 0-6-0 Jinty Tank acting as Mill Street shunter. The signal box on the right is Wolverhampton No. 2.

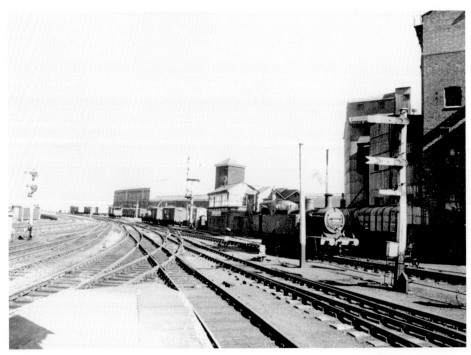

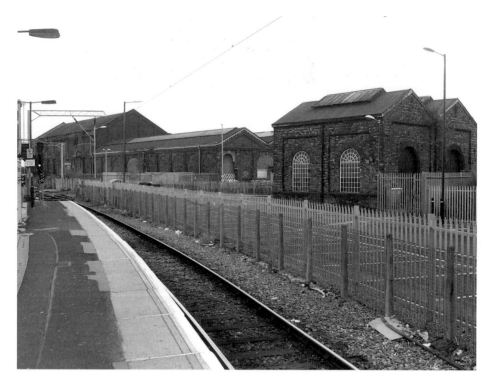

High Level Station 2011

Above is the south end of High Level station in 2011. Mill Street goods yard has long gone, as has No. 2 signal box. However, some of the old buildings still remain in a derelict condition. The lower view shows new covered stairways linking the platforms.

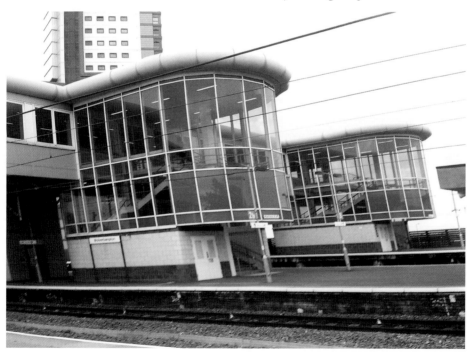

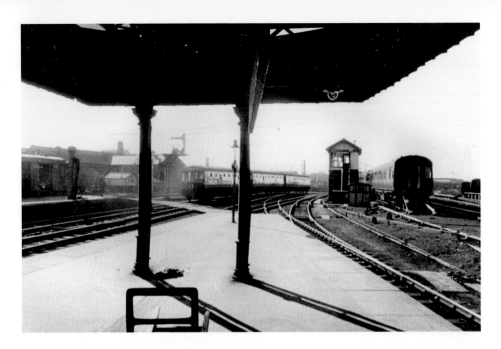

High Level Station

The northern end of the High Level station in 1960 with a DMU approaching. Also in view is a Wolverhampton No. 3 signal box and the 11 road carriage shed. In 2011, new covered staircases have replaced the old scene. The carriage sidings and No. 3 signal box have gone and diesel traction has mostly been replaced by electric services as the overhead wires testify. However, several services are diesel hauled.

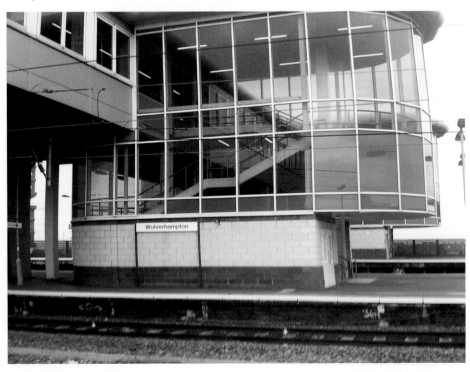

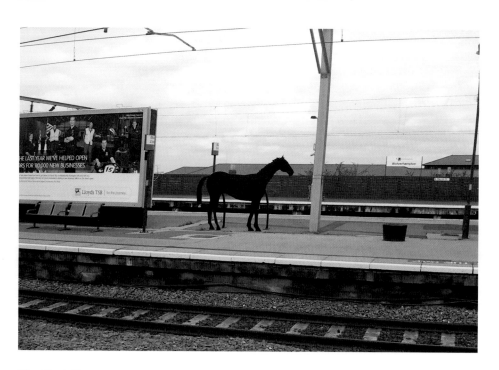

The Black Horse

The black horse at the end of Birmingham High Level station. These horses were introduced on the line to New Street when the new station was built and several still exist on the Stour Valley line. Below is Wolverhampton power signal box, replacing many of the old ones which existed in steam days.

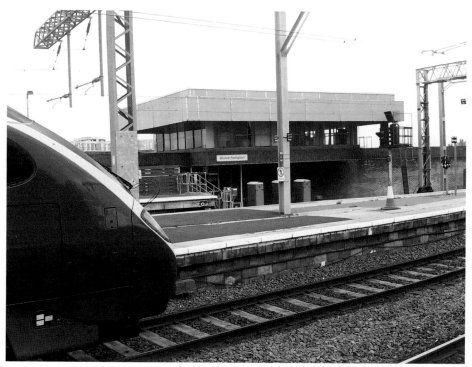

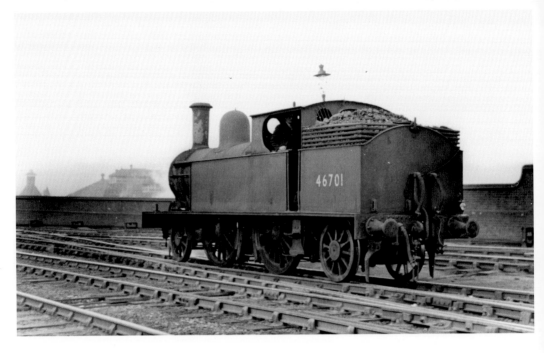

Ex-LNWR 2-4-2T No. 46701

Above, No. 46701 prepares to collect its motor train and propel it into High Level station with a service for Walsall. The engine is seen at Littles Lane Bridge on 30 April 1952. Below, the two-coach motor train is running back into High Level station after the 2-4-2 has coupled up. The locomotive is standing in for 2-6-2T No. 41229 which is in works.

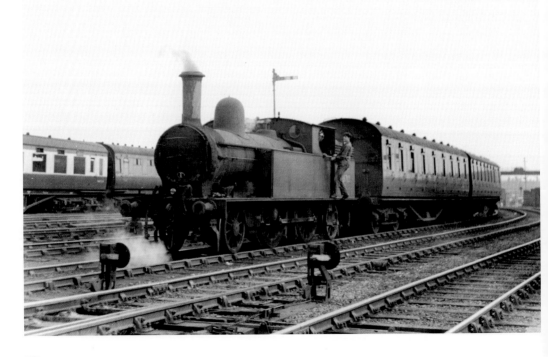

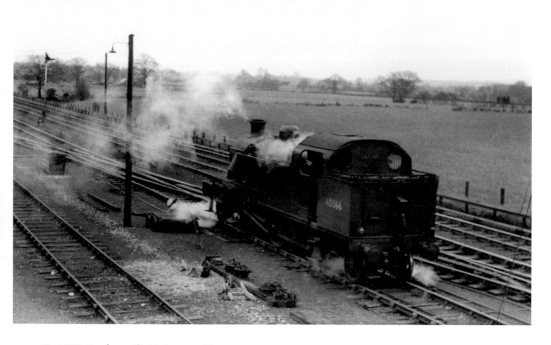

Ex-LMS Fowler 2-6-2T No. 40066

On 21 March 1952, ex-LMS Fowler 2-6-2T No. 40066 is at Fordhouses having brought in the Euston inspector's saloon. The engine and saloon are seen later leaving Fordhouses.

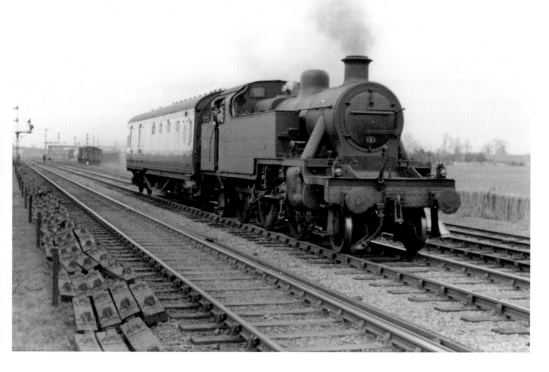

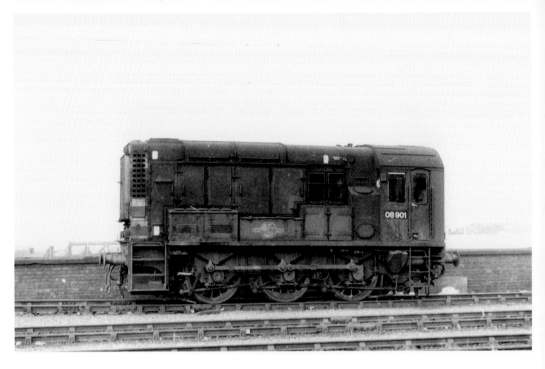

Modern Traction

By 1974, modern traction has definitely appeared at High Level. The top view shows a Class 08 0-6-0 shunter, still with the BR 'Lion and Wheel' totem, which was replaced by the arrow symbol carried on the electric loco. No. 86 246, waiting for its turn of duty at High Level, below.

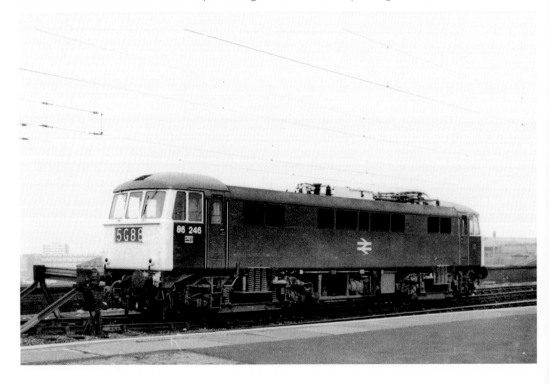

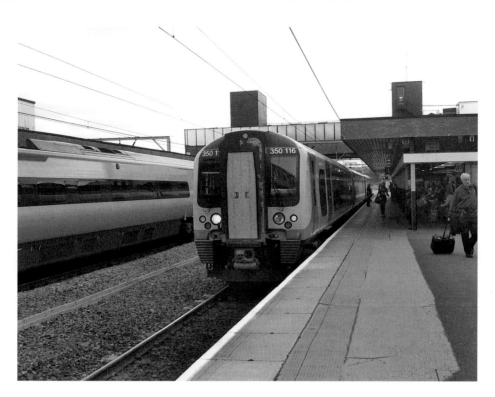

High Level Station 2011

High Level station in 2011 with, above, an electric service to Liverpool Lime Street and, below, another electric service to Birmingham New Street, calling at Sandwell and Dudley only.

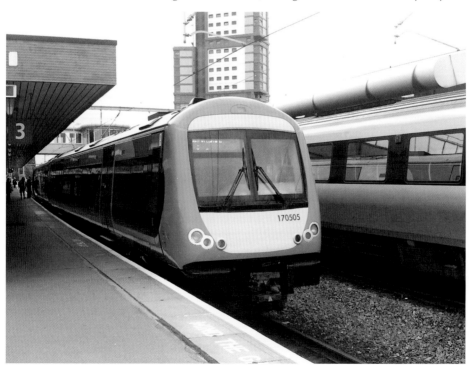

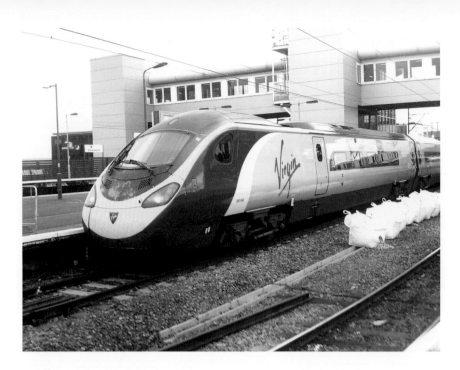

Virgin Pendelino Trains

Two views of Virgin Railways' Pendelino trains which operate between Scotland and Euston, via Wolverhampton and Birmingham. Since privatisation, several companies operate services through Wolverhampton, including Virgin Trains and London Midland. The latter tends to run services from Euston to Liverpool and Manchester. They also operate many of the West Midland local services. Today, Wolverhampton station is operated by Network Rail who took over from Railtrack when it went broke.

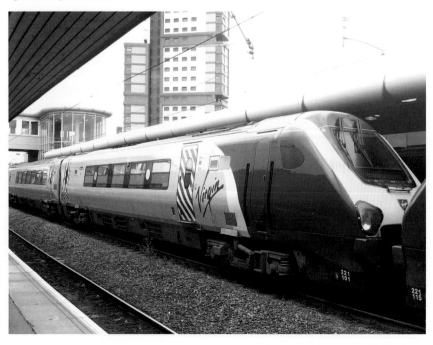

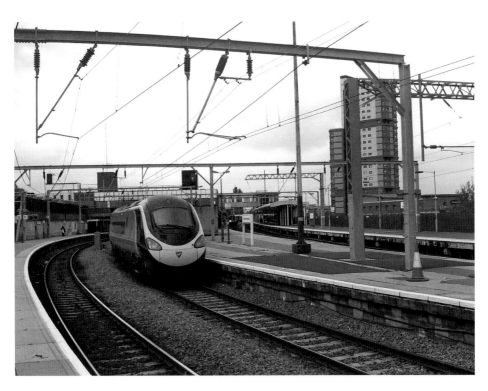

Wolverhampton High Level, Looking North
Two views of Wolverhampton High Level, looking north with Pendelino and local London Midland trains in view.

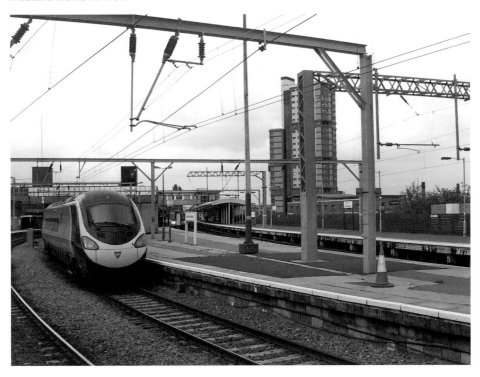

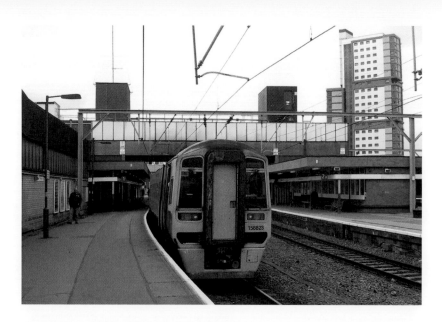

Birmingham International to Holyhead

The top view shows an Arriva Trains Wales service from Birmingham International to Holyhead. Ironically, the train follows the route which was planned by the LNWR and S&B – from Birmingham New Street, along the Stour Valley line to High Level, thence to Shrewsbury along the S&B line to connect with the Shrewsbury and Chester Railway for access to Chester and then to North Wales and Birkenhead and the Mersey. Had the Euston company not been so belligerent in its dealings with the small, but stout, S&B and S&C then the LNWR would have had a monopoly of traffic to both sides of the Mersey instead of forcing the Shrewsbury companies into the hands of the GWR. Below is a Virgin CrossCountry service to Manchester.

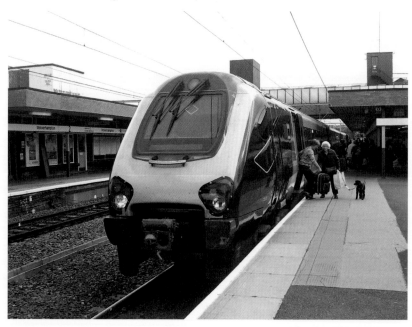

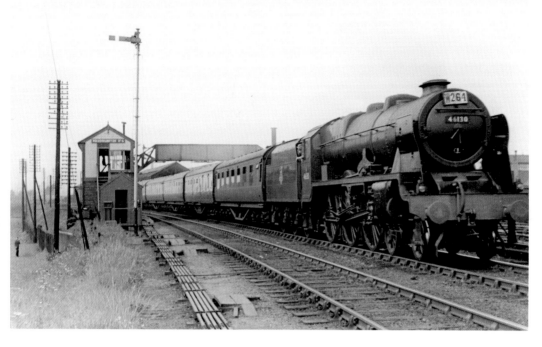

The West Yorkshire Regiment and E. C. T. French

Top is ex-LMS rebuilt Royal Scot Class 4-6-0 No. 46130 *The West Yorkshire Regiment* on a southbound train as it enters Wolverhampton on 30 June 1951 with Wolverhampton No. 4 box to the left. Below, ex-LMS Patriot Class 4-6-0 No. 45539 *E. C. T. French* is passing Fordhouses sidings with a southbound train.

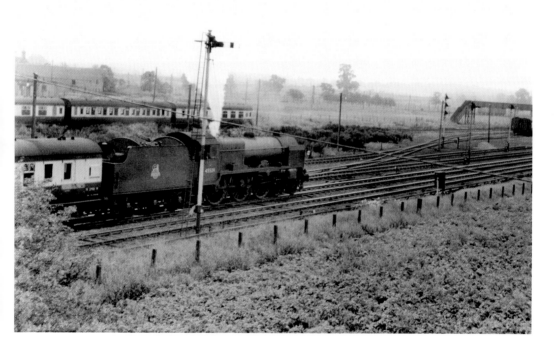

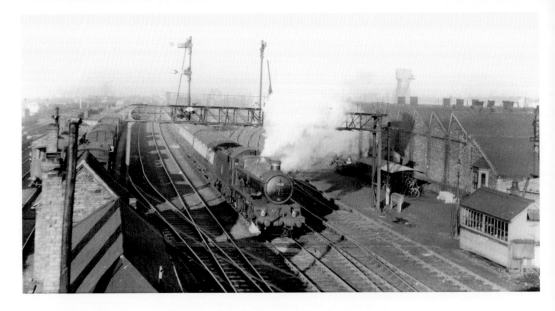

Kingswear Castle

Above is an usual sight with ex-GWR Castle Class 4-6-0 No. 5015 *Kingswear Castle* passing the ex-LNWR locoshed at Bushbury on 29 November 1953. The train had been diverted from its usual Birkenhead to Birmingham Snow Hill route due to work at Shifnal. The train travelled to Wellington, thence to Stafford and Bushbury Junction (over ex-LNWR metals) to join the line down to Low Level. Given the history between the GWR and LNWR this was an unusual sight indeed. Below at Bushbury shed is ex-MR 0-6-0 No. 58183 on 15 January 1952.

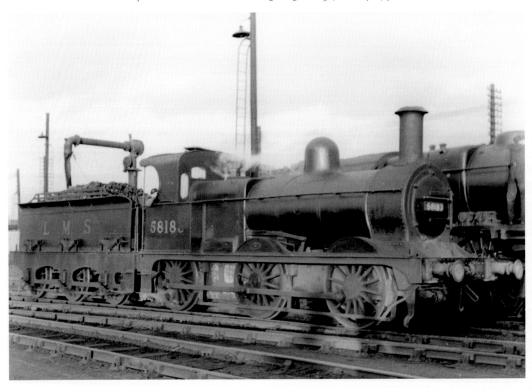

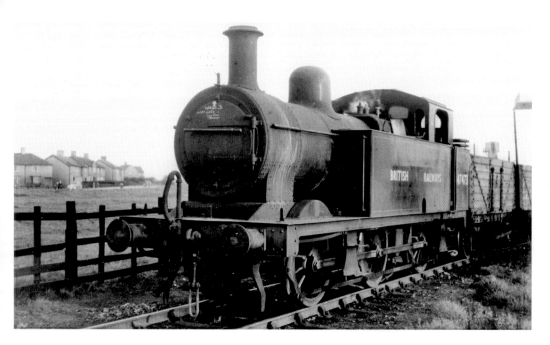

Bushbury Coaling Plant
Near the turntable at Bushbury
on 1 May 1949 is ex-LMS 0-6-0T
No. 47473. The loco. is on
coaling duties as the coaling
plant is under repair. The
engine has the legend 'Wolves
3 Leicester 1' on the smokebox
door, relating to the FA Cup
Final of 30 April 1949 and
includes a sprig of vegetation
on the upper lamp bracket.
Below is the coaling plant in
question on 30 July 1947.

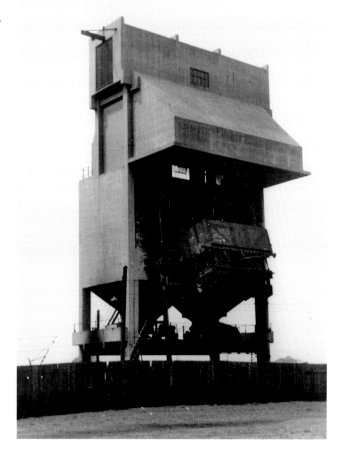

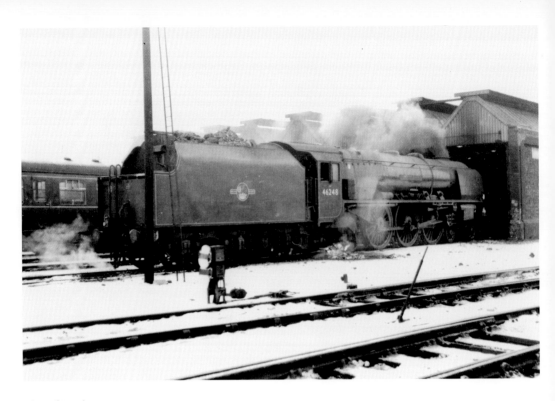

City of Leeds
Two views of locos at Bushbury shed during the winter of 1962. Above is ex-LMS Stanier Princess Coronation Pacific No. 46248 *City of Leeds* an unusual sight at Bushbury, while below is a more humble ex-LNWR Super D 0-8-0 freight engine No. 49452.

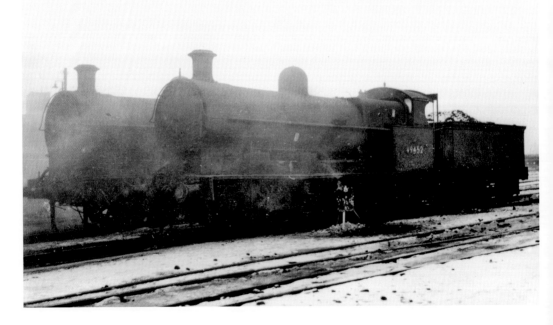

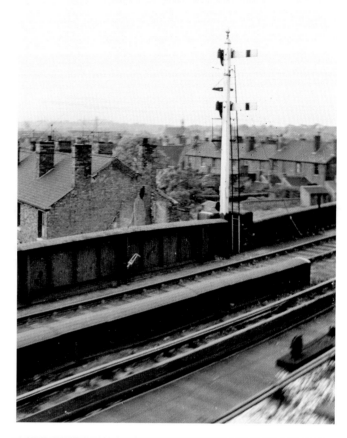

Walsall and Wednesfield
A pair of home signals on the
ex-MR line to Walsall in 1957
situated on the bridge in the
Heath Town area. Below is
the ex-MR Wednesfield goods
depot in the late 1950s with a
pair of ex-LNWR Super
D 0-8-0s of Bescot shed on
duty.

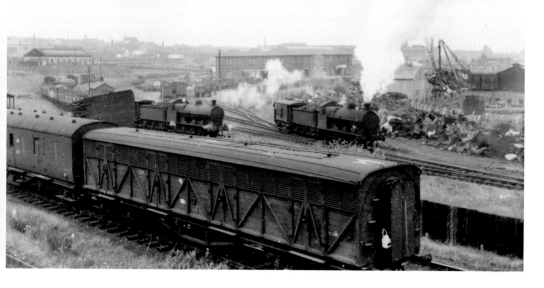

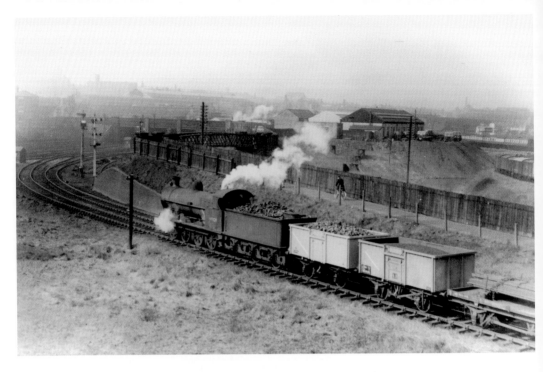

Wednesfield Goods Yard
Views approaching Wednesfield goods yard on 20 March 1955 with Super D No. 49238 on a diverted goods run down to the GWR Low Level station. The lower view shows an ex-GWR railmotor train on the left and High Level station can be seen in the distance.

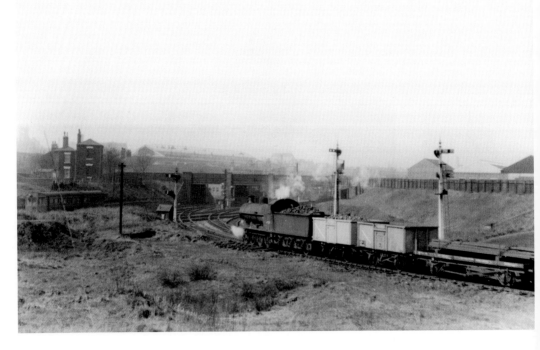

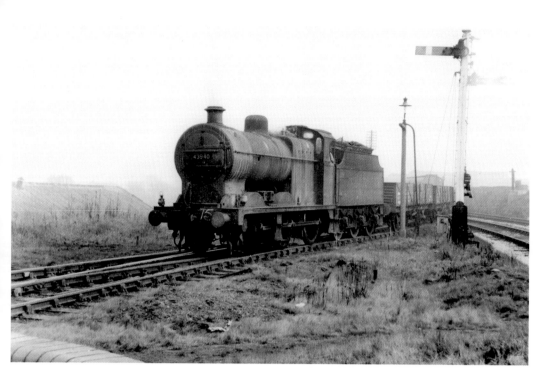

Wednesfield Goods Yard

Entering Wednesfield goods yard on 13 February 1964 is ex-LMS 4F 0-6-0 No. 43940 with the 9.35 a.m. goods from Water Orton, while below is Super D No. 48895 on shunting duty at the yard on same day.

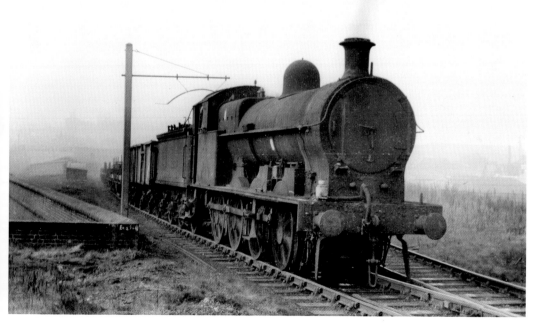

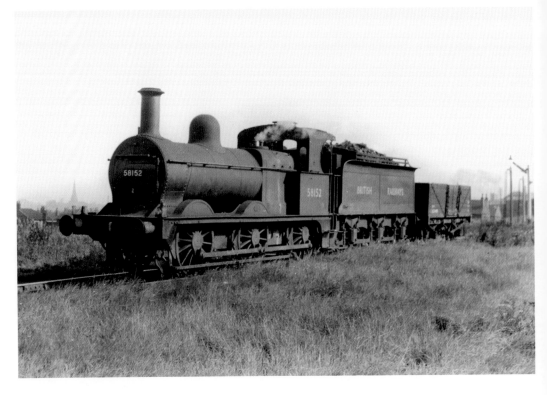

Wednesfield Goods Yard

Bushburys ex-MR 0-6-0 No. 58152 shunts in Wednesfield yard on 19 September 1952, while below, more modern traction in the shape of BR 2-6-0 No. 76039 is shunting in the yard on 21 October 1965.

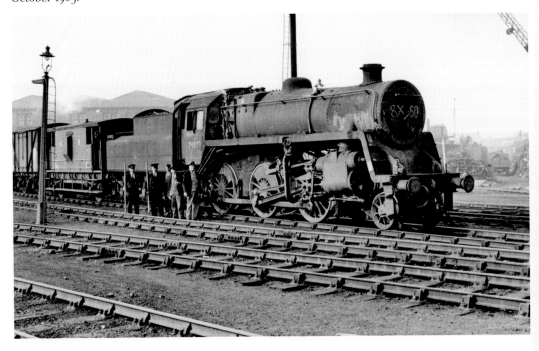

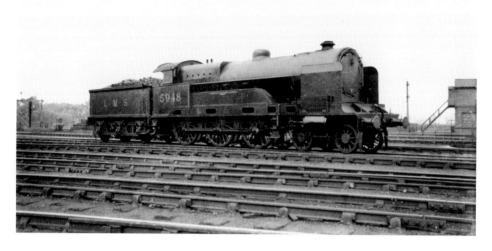

Bescot Yard

The major yard at Bescot which was opened by the LNWR in 1892 and still serves the freight network in this area and remains busy. Above is ex-LNWR Claughton Class 4-6-0 as LMS No. 5948 *Baltic* at Bescot yard on 18 August 1935. As can be seen in the 2011 view below, Bescot yard remains busy with plenty of wagons in view. Much of the freight work today is container traffic which has come in from abroad.

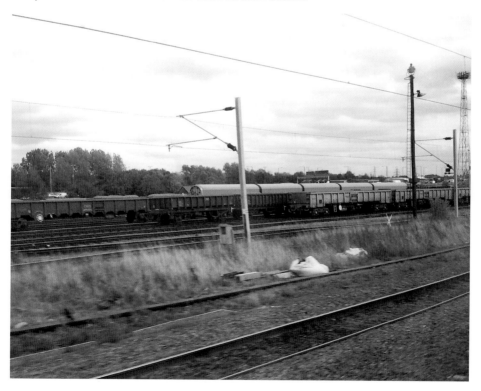

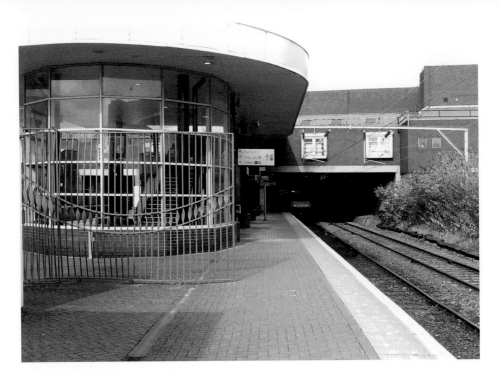

Walsall Station

Two views of Walsall station in September 2011. This was the junction of the MR line from Wolverhampton and the South Staffordshire line of the LNWR from Dudley. The old LNWR line continues through the tunnel through Bloxwich and joins the Trent Valley line at Lichfield.

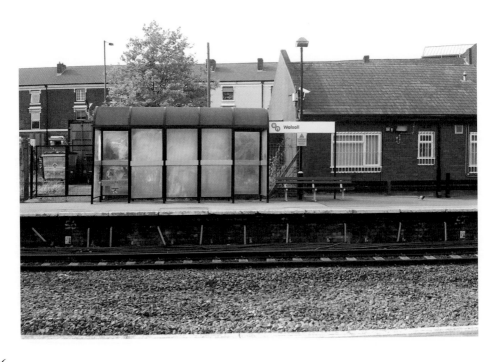

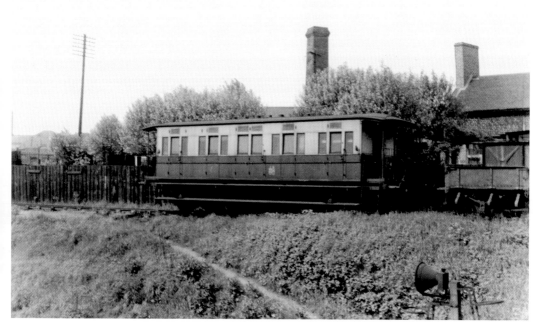

Coaches

Along with locomotives, there was a great variety of coaching stock which made up trains at Wolverhampton. Above is an ex-GWR engineer's saloon at Cannock Road sidings on 27 May 1952. Below is an ex-LMS Brake Open Third-Class coach at Fordhouses siding on 27 April 1956.

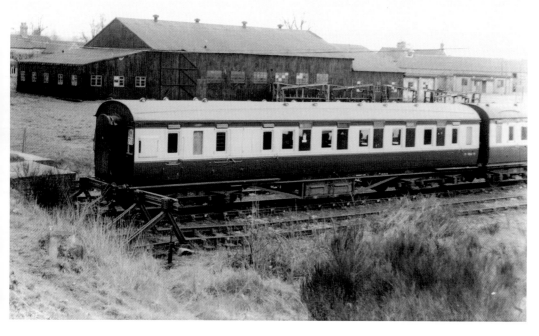

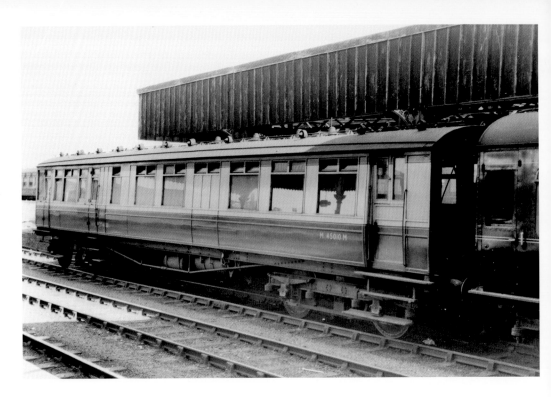

Coaches

The upper view shows an ex-LMS inspector's saloon at the rear of a train from Crewe at High Level station on 9 July 1958. Below is a 1921 Wolverton-built coach in blue livery at High Level station on 5 July 1975.

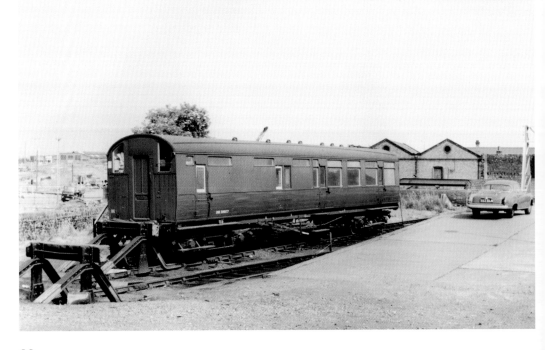

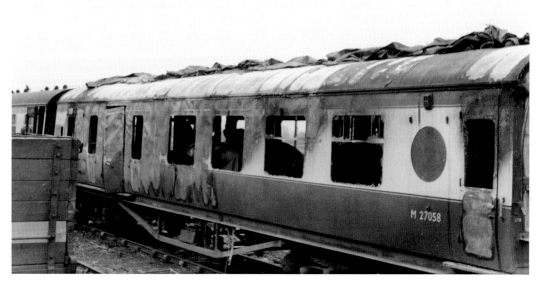

Burned-out Coaches
Burned-out coaches at Fordhouses sidings on 21 March 1952.

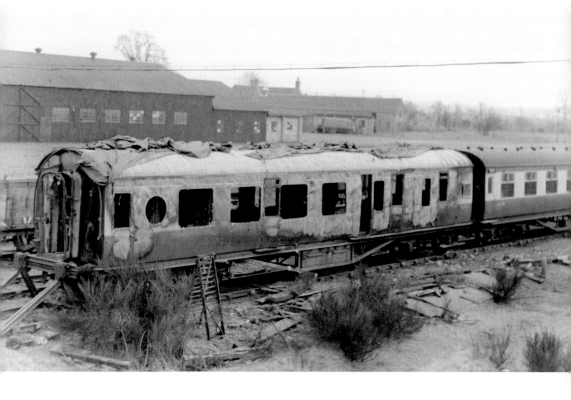

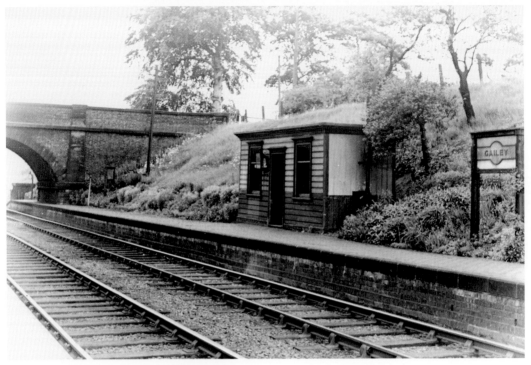

Gailey Station

Gailey station on its last working day, 16 July 1951. Above is a general view of the station with the bridge carrying the Roman Watling Street on the left and, below, Stationmistress Mrs Rooke (in the centre) is taking tickets for the final time.

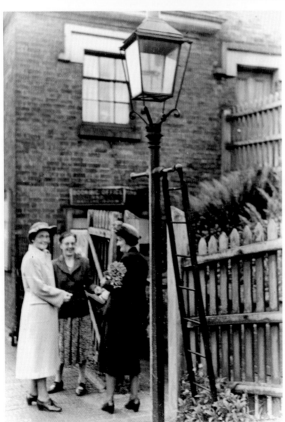

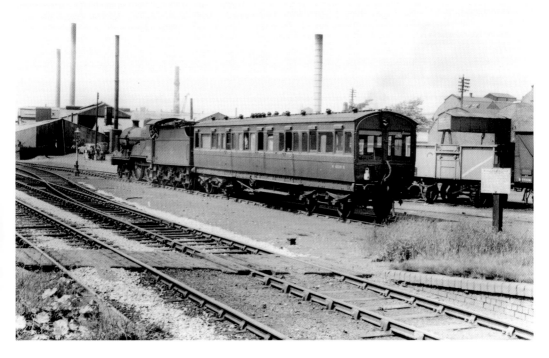

Wednesfield and Stour Valley

At the old MR Wednesfield station is ex-MR 2P 4-4-0 No. 40692 with an ex-LYR Inspector's saloon on 10 July 1958. Below is the Stour Valley station at Wednesfield in 1965.

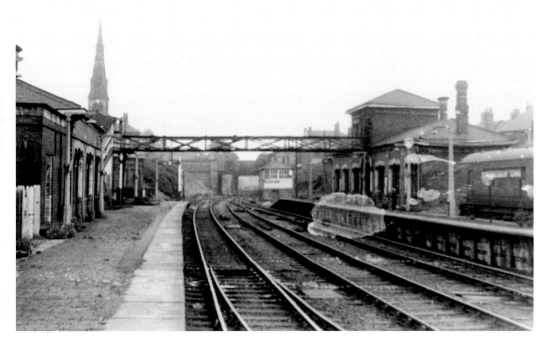

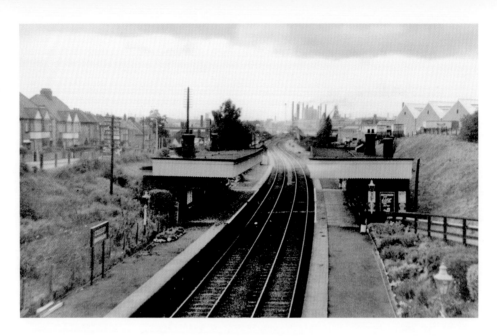

Coseley and Spon Lane

The stations at Coseley and Spon Lane on the Stour Valley Line. Originally authorised as the Birmingham, Wolverhampton & Stour Valley Railway in 1846, it was only a small part of a scheme envisaged by the S&B who had projected a line from Smethwick and through the Stour Valley to Stourbridge and Stourport to connect with the River Severn. The 'Stour Valley' tag was superfluous as the line never ran as far as the valley of the Stour. What was eventually approved was a line from Birmingham New Street to Bushbury and a junction with the GJR. There was also a plan to build a branch to Dudley. As the line linked the GJR with the London & Birmingham Railway, the SVR was under the control of the LNWR from the start. The SVR was complete by 1850, but the LNWR refused to open it as a way of preventing the GWR from gaining access to it. The Euston company also did everything it could to keep the S&B out, even though they had a share. It was this prevention of use of the SVR, along with some illegal LNWR practices which brought the S&B and S&C into GWR orbit.

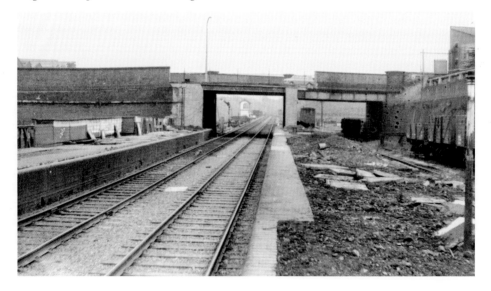

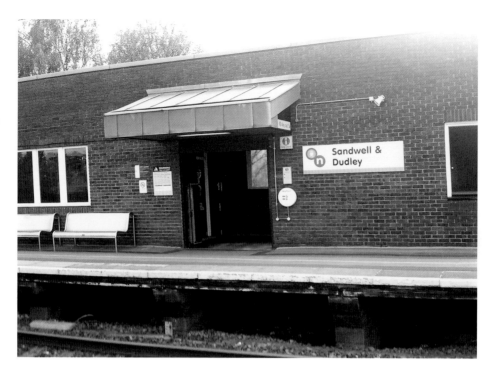

Sandwell and Dudley

Sandwell and Dudley station in 2011. The old LNWR station of Dudley Port, famous for LNWR 2-4-2T locomotives, seen here at the head of local trains down to the South Staffs and OW&W station at Dudley. Sadly, Dudley has long since closed and Sandwell and Dudley station is now the only station to serve the town, which has a bus connection.

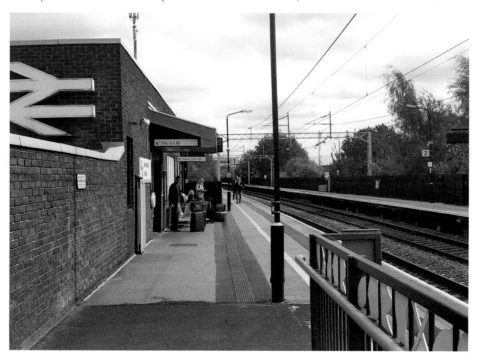

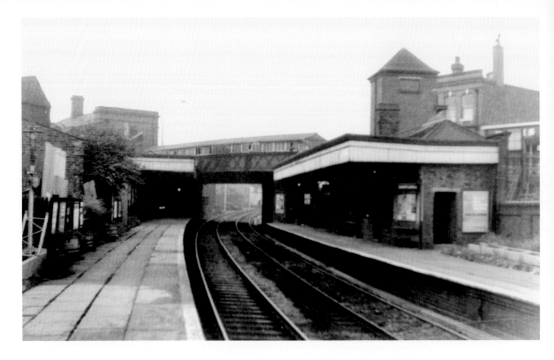

Smethwick Stations

The upper view shows Smethwick station on the Stour Valley line, now Smethwick Rolfe Street. Below, a new station, Smethwick Galton Bridge, which is an interchange between the SVR and ex-GWR line to Stourbridge and Kidderminster from Birmingham Snow Hill, has opened. Its station name is seen here.

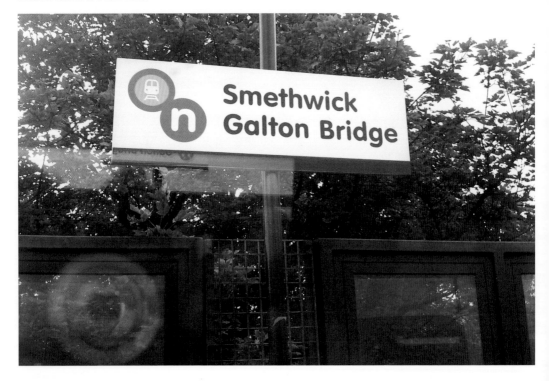

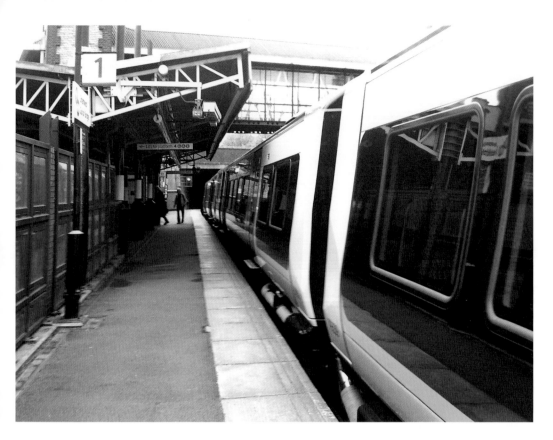

Lady Godiva

The upper view shows Smethwick Galton Bridge station on the ex-GWR Snow Hill-Stourbridge Junction line. Below, on 27 April 1947, LMS Patriot 4-6-0 No. 5519 *Lady Godiva* has been derailed at the north end of Bushbury sidings.

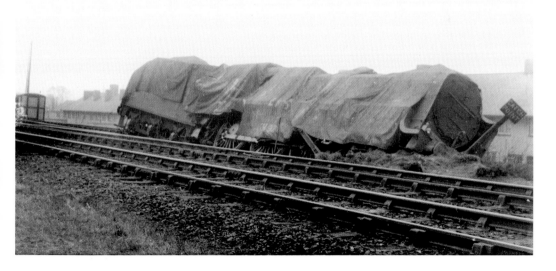

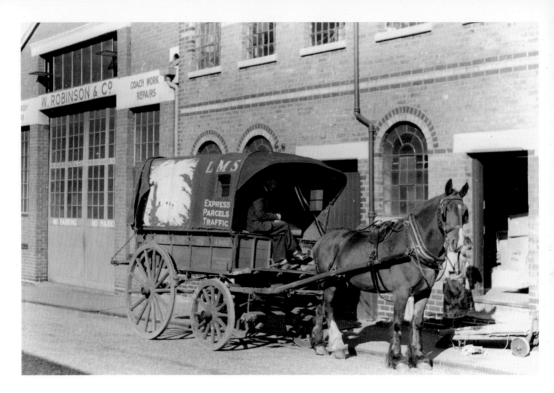

Changing Times

Back at Wolverhampton on 18 September 1952 and a horse-drawn cart is delivering parcels which have arrived from the station. Much has changed since those days. Firstly, delivery by horse and cart was unusual even in 1952, let alone a cart still carrying the 'LMS' legend. Secondly most deliveries would now come by lorry rather than railway today, which has done much to damage rail freight traffic and clog up the roads. Finally, such factories as the one in this view have long disappeared as the country has abandoned its industrial past and chosen to import its needs – and then everyone wonders why we have a balance of payments deficit and the country no longer produces anything which would keep people in employment.

Acknowledgements

I have enjoyed exploring the railway history of Wolverhampton as well as riding on trains and experiencing the new tramway system between Birmingham Snow Hill and Wolverhampton. The latter is a good way to travel and National Express needs to be congratulated on such an excellent system, along with the councils involved. Thanks now go to those who have helped with this project, not least Roger Carpenter, LOSA, and David Ibbotson.

Thanks also go to Wolverhampton library and the *Wolverhampton Express and Star*. Many thanks to my brother Paul and his partner Roma for allowing me to stay in their home while I undertook this work and to my wife Hilary who keeps me in cups of tea while I carry on with the work.